AF504126

Bollywood: An Insider's Guide

Fuad Omar

Mayhem Publishing
London

Bollywood: An Insider's Guide
Copyright © Fuad Omar 2006

All Rights Reserved

No part of this book may be reproduced in any form by
photocopying or by electronic or mechanical means, including
information storage or retrieval systems, without permission in
writing from both the copyright owner and the publisher of this book.

Cover Design: Ray Nivana

First Published 2006 by Mayhem Publishing, London

CONTENTS

Bollywood: An Insider's Guide

Fuad Omar

Introduction

I owe my life to Bollywood. This is a bold statement by any standards, implying that some kind of blood-debt or miraculous event must have occurred which makes me say that my life is owed to a film industry.

As long as I can remember, I have loved moving pictures. Not *films*, but moving pictures. Be it the lantern with cuts in its embracing shade that twirls round to make a shadowy figure dance entertaining the child I used to be or a simple flick book that uses the same principle as stop-motion animation and allows a series of still images to become an animated short, I simply *love* moving pictures.

Add a dash of colour, twists in the story, songs and dances that celebrate all life has to celebrate, sprinkle in some humour and a moment of action and you have the greatest story telling machine in the world. What I particularly liked about Hindi films was that they weren't in English. I was watching rented VHS tapes of the latest Indian movies at a family friends house (we couldn't afford a VCR) in Harrow and I loved that these films had the audacity to be in the same language I speak at home as opposed to the one I'm taught at school. Of course, at that young age I didn't know these were "Indian" films, they were simply films I had the most exposure to and they were theatrical in their running times and in their doses of melodrama. Amitabh Bachchan would appear in almost every film and occasionally we'd watch a film with a pale-faced Shammi Kapoor who spent much of his screen time prancing around yelping in gardens, mountains and around lakes. This was when I first knew I loved moving pictures and that I loved Bollywood.

After having written some 300-plus articles, it was difficult to select a few for this unique collection. My first criteria would be that I would revisit the source of my articles: my notes before the interview, my original first drafts and the ones I felt would present an overall glimpse of my experience with Bollywood. Some readers of this collection will have heard of me through my work with Asian Xpress, Asiangigs or The Times, but to others this may be the first time you're reading my work. The aim of this collection is to entice everyone – the casual Bollywood fan, the devotee and the newbie (who simply finds the world of Indian cinema fascinating but knows little more about it).

In this collection you will find printed for the first time, full interviews devoid of the editing process that makes an article fit for publication. Gone are the restraints of numbers and column spaces and so you'll find very long interviews with the likes of Shah Rukh Khan, Hrithik Roshan and Sushmita Sen (as well as a host of others). You'll also find my notes on Kabhi Khushi Kabhie Gham's set visits as well as the final text which appeared in the Asian Xpress weeks before the film released. There will be on-set reports, film reviews and reviews of live shows, as well as general articles about your favourite celebrity or Bollywood.

Since the majority of feedback to my work was generated through my *Insider* column in the Asian Xpress, I've chosen to call this book Bollywood: An Insider's Guide, which will take the fan beyond the silver screen and into the world they do not often get to see behind the curtain. Here you'll find the people behind the personalities, the dedication and hard work that goes into making three hour opuses (some of which bomb on the day of release discarding three years of hard work) and much more.

Bollywood has always been a big part of my life and always will be. As I write this introduction, I'm recovering from covering the UK leg of a frantic Bollywood world tour and preparing for work on a film that is likely to be the most eagerly anticipated moving picture of 2006. The experience is exhausting, adrenalized and inspiring… and I hope it never ends.

Welcome to Bollywood. I'll be your tour guide. Enjoy the ride.

Fuad Omar
May 2006

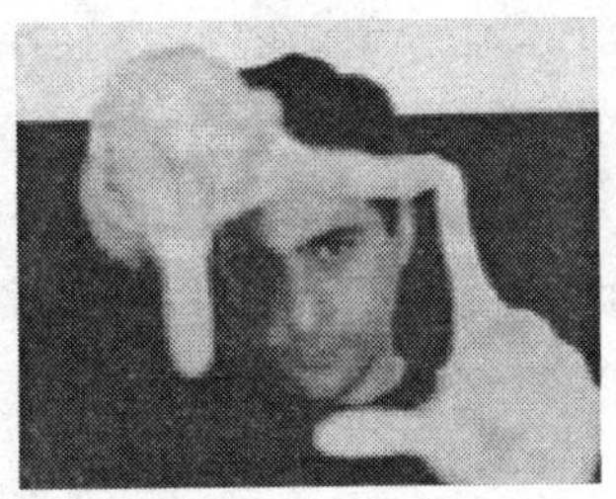

BOLLYWOOD: BEHIND THE GLAMOUR

As I write this I'm celebrating an anniversary. As I type away with fingers hitting keys causing that inevitable flutter-shutter sound, it's been approximately one year since my first piece for Asian Xpress.

The past year has had its ups and downs and its in-betweens, but mostly it's just been one wild ride. The first piece I had with the paper was the now infamous Hrithik Roshan interview, which many of you wrote in to give feedback on months later when I announced my column and gave an email address. I had just finished what was a month long schedule with Karan Johar and crew for the mammoth production of Kabhi Khushi Kabhie Ghum, and was experiencing my own form of melancholy because after a lot of good times, masti, hard work and unplanned excitement that always accompanies film shoots, I was really missing my friends in the cast and crew. Waking up at the crack of dawn (sometimes when it should be always), to get to where the crew are shooting before set up or the first shot, speaking to a crew member for directions only to be told, 'How can you not find us? We've put signs up everywhere and all the way', only to find the most miniscule and obscure looking signs (one simply had the letter 'K' and an arrow) and to discover I have no sense of road directions whatsoever. The K3G shoot was probably the most memorable one I've been on, because I was in the company of friends.

Karan is not only a dear friend, but also an amazing director and to watch him at work is like watching a ticking time-bomb waiting to explode. Some of the observations I made during that shoot of just how he works could fill a book, but then most observations on most shoots could. From seeing the Yeh Ladki Hai Allah song being picturised the night of the Filmfares in what should have seemed like the dead of night but seemed more like a lively wedding in a small basti at Film City, to holding back tears of laughter watching Shah Rukh and Kajol shoot at Mychett Place in Surrey as they enacted the married couple scenes, it certainly still brings a smile to my face.

This week's spread is for you. For the fans of Indian cinema, for the readers of my column and work to say thank you, reminisce and share with you some experiences that are a slice straight from my own life, showing you what lies behind the glamorous industry you all see and love, and sometimes laugh at.

Many of you write to me regularly, sometimes asking for information, mostly to give feedback (and it's all appreciated thanks) and occasionally I get emails from people wanting advice on getting into the industry, or wanting to shadow me and see what it's like being a Bollywood journalist and so let me talk you through some of the shenanigans you have to go through that end up making it as a sentence in an article somewhere.

Bollywood is the name given to the Indian film industry and I literally have loathed that word from day one. It's too camp and similar to Hollywood in sound, in fact it's a direct derivation of the term. It implies the Indian film industry is a cheap imitation or wannabe second rate version of Hollywood, which is not the case. In fact, historically speaking India was making films way before its American counterparts and so we should say they're copying us! But enough of the banter, I put up with the term and moved on. Bollywood is a completely different world from the place we live in. There are characters, genuine people, hopefuls, technically brilliant minded individuals and amazing families. There are also a lot of parties, many fake people (read as having to be courteous) and hours that come from within other hours of the day. The Indian film industry is anything but glamorous. It looks great on-screen but to create that perfect image takes a lot of people, a lot of time and a whole lot of effort and retakes. Yes every heroine looks beautiful and every man looks idealistic, but that's what the industry is there to do: sell dreams.

Even in the photos everyone looks perfect, carrying off the most absurd of costumes with panache and style and without a morsel of regret, and you think these people have it easy. I've heard it many times: people come up to you and say how easy it is to be an actor in Indian cinema and how all you have to do is have make up put on, perform a few really easy lines and dance with beautiful girls. You wish. It's extremely tough and the hours are gruelling, the pressure immense and it's true when they say 'every Friday holds someone's fortune' because when a film that's taken years to complete finally makes it onto the big screen, it only takes three shows in the first day to decide it and its stars fates.

An actress I know very well was shooting for two films one weekend and was leaving for shows the following day. She woke up and was on set by 5am, make up took two hours almost, she began the shot not before midday and wrapped up only two scenes by 6pm, was scurried by car to another location and walked into another film set, knackered as can be and began mouthing dialogues of a completely different character within seconds as she was being made up for a different film. She finished at 3am, went home to finish packing for the shows she's meant to depart for in less than six hours and while she was packing and instructing friends what would need to be taken in which suitcase, a dress designer came round (yep at 4am) and began a costume fitting which needed to be done for a shoot for when she came back. 24 hours after her day began she was still working, having only napped in the car. On landing at the destination wearing dark glasses and smiling for everyone (because dare I say no one would understand an actress being cranky in public, after all she's not allowed to right, whatever the conditions). Greeted by hoards of fans that cause a security issue she plods through to TV cameras who want to know how it is to be on this tour and catch her while they can. She smiles and delivers an impeccably perfect two minute interview before being whisked away in a limo to the hotel where she has 3 hours to catch up on some sleep before a press conference to promote the very show she's on.

Still sound glamorous?

The only glamorous part is what you see on screen, what you don't see is the hard work that goes into making that one song look as it does. All the different costumes and locations may be made fun of at times, but each location was a plane trip away, every costume took hours to get into, forward planning and the right lighting and even then all you see are edited shots composed together from hours of footage to make it look like a wondrous song. It ain't all song and dance though. Rehearsals for shows, in between script-readings, story narrations, photo-shoots, interviews and of course, shooting, there's very little time left if you're in this mad, bad world of Bollywood.

So that's partly what some of it is like, but what about the fame, money and glory? Well it's not a secure industry because one flop and you're written off courtesy of certain journalists, so you really better make good while you're here. You can make lots of money but only with the right filmmakers and deals and if you work with the best production houses, working with them is reward enough to cause a dent in your pay packet, so what do you choose – moolah or good films? The only guarantee you have is that there is no guarantee. If you keep your head down, work hard and round the clock for a few years you may get enough bank to support your wife and kids, who you might not get to see all that much, because did I mention you're working all hours and all across the world?

But that's what the industry is: a dream factory. It produces and sells dreams to the public and they take it as escapism or entertainment that takes them away from reality or gives them hope that a better life is within reach. It's a dream factory because once you enter the industry, your eyes are full of hope and dreams and you can live out every role you wanted to as a kid everyday and have a lot of fun. Just don't think it's not hard work.

Don't get me wrong though, everyone (well almost everyone) loves it here. You think an eighteen hour shoot is a long time but when you get there and don the greasepaint, crack a laugh with your co-stars and the technicians, you actually enjoy it and make the atmosphere as pleasant as possible and time can go fast. I've yet to come across a miserable actor who regrets being in the industry, it's a great job and you can live out amazing experiences every day, I'm just saying it isn't the glamour industry many perceive it to be. So what's it like being the guy who is neither of this world nor that, but sits on the fence that is the celluloid 70mm screen and listens to the audience to report back to those behind the screen and vice versa? I'll tell you another day. But for now, Welcome to Bollywood! It's mad, it's fun and it's full of dreams, just don't give anyone a hard time because you think it's an easy job.

Fuad Omar

HRITHIK ROSHAN: PHENOMENON!

This interview marked my first article published in the Asian Xpress and received the most amount of feedback. It was quoted from across the world in various publications and to this day, seems to represent a side of Hrithik others have yet to discover. This is the first time the interview is published in its complete unedited entirety.

GENESIS

Hrithik Roshan achieved phenomenal success within the first few days of his debut film. A few months later after the filmi gossip journals had squeezed dry as many covers with the current craze, and sold many issues using his image, they began the next phase of the vicious circle that enjoins the star-filmi press relationship: they began to ask if he was a one-hit wonder and as to whether his second film would cut it and touch the heights of Kaho Naa Pyaar Hai's success. In an industry where a star is considered as hot as his last release, the press began to carry reports speculating on Hrithik's talent. Khalid Mohammed's Fiza was released to a bumper response and although did not get the success it had hoped for in India, internationally it packed cinema houses everywhere and gained Hrithik critical praise for a hauntingly realistic portrayal of a brother attempting to make sense of an non-sensical time. A few coke ads and a technically brilliant movie later, Mission Kashmir finally nailed the coffin shut which held the media's reservations about the growing young star. He had screen presence, he could act and had proved it, so for the while the howling jaws of those that pull stars down by profession are dormant.

I remember seeing Kaho Naa Pyaar Hai at a trial showing just before the film's release and carefully writing my review, predicting big things for the two newcomers if they chose their future ventures wisely and were given the opportunity to grow. This initial curiosity grew as the film became a blockbuster and Hrithik a sensation, and following his career what magnetically drew me towards wanting to interview him was that despite what was written about him and how success had come to him easily, he had struggled, and also the fact that he had given three sensitively different performances in his first three films and whether this was the growth of an actor or just the ample opportunities to showcase his diverse talent, he had certainly succeeded. Another factor was the flashes of sensitivity he used to reveal when being interviewed, be it when he was dispelling rumours which were being circulated about him or talking about his father, his responses were never hollow and always showed thought. Granted the questions he has been asked have generated similar responses from him because every journalist seems to have the same queries, but the untouched aspects of Hrithik are like a treasure chest, which will unfold with time. Determined to satisfy my curiosity in the phenomenon and how he has dealt with the immense pressure and attention he has been bestowed with, I began conjuring angles and questions in my mind for a forthcoming article. Committed to asking questions which would reveal something about the star not previously read about in any interview and aiming to present him with questions that would never be 'standard' and would actually make him think again instead of answering the usual questions, I began my journey.

That was what this interview would be: His journey.

Flashes from his journey from the beginning to the now, glimpses of the rays which brimmed with the person and not the persona and an encounter that would not waste time by dispelling rumours or even spend a moment asking about his future films. An interview not bound by any film's release date but a timeless piece which represents the person, the growing actor and the loving son.

I now will present to you, Hrithik Roshan.

REVELATIONS

Oxford's monumental Stowe School has become the cricket ground for an interschool competitive game and one man is batting his heart out for victory. The crowd cheers as he does his best, but given who this man is, they'd cheer for him anyway even if he wasn't playing the game for he has already found his way firmly into their hearts as a favourite. The game is halted (and not due to bad weather), but because another shot is to set up as cameras are shifted and players are moved. This is the set of Karan Johar's Kabhi Khushi Kabhie Gham and the one being cheered is Hrithik Roshan.

Since the UK schedule began he is forever singing in between shots and talking to those on the sets about everything from the latest songs and movies to delivering his straight faced jokes and imitating an impeccably typical British accent. Extras surround him for autographs and photos whenever possible and he happily obliges each request when he can, ensuring each one leaves with a smile as another from the crowd pushes forward hoping to be next. After lunch as another shot is prepared for which he's not required, we sit inside away from the busy goings on and begin the interview.

Having seen him at work since the UK schedule began, I had observed certain mannerisms of his and learnt of his sincere dedication for what he does. His body language reflects his demeanour at times and the effort he gives to each shot is like a reserved plasma of energy, releasing it's full force upon the trigger action of his director. And his need for self-satisfaction is shown as he runs to the monitor after each shot is canned to see how it's looking and if he can improve on it.

He is also a music lover – why else would I be hearing the songs of Lucky Ali or Bas Itna Sa Khawab Hai in between shots as he rendered whichever tune was in his head at the time.
"You're always singing," I say to him shaking my head.
"It's good to relax," he says to me with a smile.

I begin the interview by asking how he felt when days after his first release, he was hailed as a phenomenon and was being praised to the skies by the media bandwagon that usually follows this publicity blitzkrieg by ripping their chosen one to shreds, escalating the star only to make the fall harder.

"It was completely nerve-racking," he says looking down for a moment as he turns his mind back to the days of his first release.
"Because I knew it was just not the truth. Luckily for me I had the intelligence to know that what was going on was irresponsible and dishonest, because they (the press) were putting me up to levels of experienced persons in the business when I had just started with my first film, and even in that I wasn't that good."

He looks straight at me as he answers and appears as someone who has taken the blows and was hurt that he was not allowed to savour his taste of success. Whereas his face does not reflect pain, it does show sadness as he talks about his experience but this initial black hole which can easily hypnotise and suck in newcomers was one he saw as a challenge and faced head on, only to come out a winner.

"After a while it stopped bothering me because I just focused on what I knew and on my work and what I had to do. That's all I wanted to do."

I make a comment about how fame can have its trappings and become a prison, because stars are in a medium that gives them so much self-importance they can begin to forget what's really important and why they're where they are. I ask if he ever feels trapped by his fame and the position he's achieved and if he ever gets carried away by the attention given to him and the image he has compared to who he is.
He looks to his left as someone enters the tent we're sitting in, then back at me. With a deep sense of thought reflected in his brandy-coloured eyes, he leans forward slightly and delivers an answer based on his experiences and observations.

"It's very easy to get confused between the magic of the movies which makes you look invincible on screen and who you are in reality. It's very easy to get confused between the person you are and the persona you're projected as on screen, especially for people who've come from outside the industry. But for me I've always treated it like a job and nothing more than that," he says thoughtfully.

Hrithik places his cellular phone on the table and lifts his head a little as he eases back into his chair, getting comfortable as he continues. He's wearing a blue denim jacket with the ripped effect and jeans to match, and I thank my lucky stars my job doesn't require me to have as many different costume changes as his.

"You do your job and come back home and you are what you are when the camera's off. When the camera's on you're playing a character and that's not you. It's a character that's conceived by another person, the words he speaks are given to him by another person and he's not really bashing up the ten goons and is not really the superman he is on screen," he analyses wisely.

"But on screen that's what it looks like and so people start believing that he's that strong and can bash up ten people at one time. If it's all new to you and you're from outside the industry, you start believing that 'yes I am that person who's standing on that banner' or 'I am that romantic guy'. You start developing a fake covering all over you and you get an attitude and start walking with a little heaviness in your face like 'I'm too good'."

As he says this he uses those piercing eyes and characteristic face to mimic how someone with attitude would glance at someone, narrowing his field of vision to be as restricted as a person who believed they lived in a self created bubble where they were the only person who matters. His answer is one which seems to depict an aspect he has already dealt with, as once half the world start screaming for you and the scribes describe you as hot property, it would be only human to believe you are the epitome of popularity people are painting you to be. But as he continues it's evident this is an aspect he has dealt with, but not fallen prey to.

"But that only happens when you don't really know what it's all about and soon enough everybody realises, in a matter of time be it two years, five years or six years, that

'I am not that guy'. They are not in love with me. They are in love with the person they see on film in the theatre. It's not me saying those lines to the heroine and it's not you because that's not the person you are. They're not in love with me, they're in love with Rohit or Raj or Aman who whoever I'm playing. It's not really me and I have the intelligence to know that. So for me it was not a big problem because I never believed it. It's just a compliment when they like my work."

His answer is well thought, but I still probe and wonder as to whether the adulation has swayed him. After all, if a crowd the size of Wembley Arena are shouting his name doesn't he feel the self-importance prodding him to believe these people love the real him?

"I know that if even one person from that crowd of 80,000 or however many people there may be in an audience, had to meet me alone like in a restaurant or somewhere. They'd just come up to me and shake my hand and say 'hey you did good work, well done. We love you. Keep up the good work.' That's it, it's just a compliment and that's how I take it. There's no reason to start thinking that 'they're crazy about me' or 'I'm too good' because it's not about you it's about your work. It's about your product and your job. You do your job and as long as you do it well they love you. The moment you give a bad performance, it's over. So I never really get trapped by that, sometimes you do start thinking 'I must be that good' but it's not true it's just a job."

Impressed with his answer and the maturity with which he seems to have handled his fame, I find the interview gearing itself towards promise as the curiosity with which I had approached him begins to be satisfied and my interest remains piqued. Hrithik is not only a good actor and performer, but also someone who seems to have a strong passion for his medium, and is attempting to see shortcomings before they arrive, such as the star-trappings and a saturation point, as is evident with the roles he has done and is taking on. His perspective of his role in the industry as someone who's merely 'doing his job' has clearly helped keep his level head and the star who should categorically be the most arrogant given the success and popularity he has, is as down to earth as the next person.

An impression of Hrithik from his early Kaho Naa Pyaar Hai days up until now is that he has been constantly travelling on a continuos journey. From being an assistant to achieving super success with one film, maintaining the support of his fans and dealing with the controversies which were tossed at him, it's been a bumpy ride but a constant journey. I ask him to share with me a few of his favourite stops during this ride and recall some memorable moments.

"I think a really good decision for me was to join my father as an assistant because it really helped me a lot. I spent six years of my life behind the camera watching the best actors at work and one of the best directors at work - my father. So I got to learn so much," he says again looking at me with eyes that show respect at his father's name.

The man I came to interview and is extremely popular suddenly appears to me as his father's son and nothing more. His eyes are so full of affection for his father and his voice becomes softer, with a look that conveys deep gratitude and complete devotion. His body language also begins to relate this as he lowers his hands and leans forward, as though he is speaking of the most precious person in the world to him that it deserves that extra measure of care and respect.

He pauses before continuing, probably stealing a moment to think of his father again, before going on and returning to his answer.

"It was good for me as far as my career is concerned but it was also hell being there physically. There were times when I had to go without food, or sleep for only four hours and all the running around I had to do as an assistant was tough work. I had to bath in brown water sometimes, the conditions were terrible because my father was into action films and was shooting in deserts and jungles, but I got to learn a lot," he says reminiscing, telling how he has struggled rather than being someone who found success easily.

The only reason his struggle and hard work has been masked at times is because he is often portrayed as someone who was born as he is, gifted a dream debut which was tailored to highlight him and has fallen into stardom by chance. Sound stunningly familiar of your favourite filmi gossip mag? Don't believe the hype.

"Working as an assistant helped my decision to be an actor and take the final plunge by joining the classes of Kishore Kapoor and get my photosession done by Daboo Ratnani, and then to get the offer from dad was so unexpected. I always thought my first film would be with somebody else and not my father, because I knew he would not compromise, he would not take me just because I`m his son. So when he offered me this film it was the best compliment I could ever get. Because I knew he would only take me if he thought I was good enough for it and at that meant I was good enough. So that really was a memorable time," he says recalling his spark of interest which stems from his early days, only to become an engulfing inferno of determination, passion and enthusiasm which would push him to become the name he is today.

"Then of course my training was another memorable time. The time I spent with Salman was amazing and really helped me a lot. And then every day of shooting Kaho Naa Pyaar Hai, every second was a learning experience where I picked so much information, and it was great fun," he says with a smile, again shifting in his chair and listening carefully to my next point.

Hrithik is not the star son who received everything on a golden platter. His father may be a respected actor and filmmaker, but at the time of his son's launch he was not considered a legend by any means, just a simple man who did good work. Hrithik's arrival was a star's son's launch but it wasn't such a big star's launch that everyone could announce beforehand they expected him to do well because of what has been given to him.

"Especially in this career you cannot be handed anything because the logic just does not apply. Ultimately you stand on your own and there are so many star sons who have come and received opportunities but if you're not good enough or you don't deserve it, you're just turned away and you end up worse than what you started off with. You lose your individuality and you become known as a flop actor and people pass remarks about you, so it's a really big risk with your life."

EXODUS

As we approach the next chronicle of his journey, I take a minute to pause and ask him about the future before moving on, and ask if like the dream he once had to act, another exists or is weaving in his mind to direct. Something one would expect from someone whose life has unfolded on the sets and been eternally bonded with the visual medium.

"Right now I just want to take one shot at a time and put everything into every shot. I do want to direct some day, but I don't know if I'll have the guts to do it. I just need to mature a bit more, experience life a little more because to be a director you really need to understand human behaviour. You need to have seen a lot in life and I think maybe in time I will," he says as he loses himself in his thoughts, seemingly dreaming of a tomorrow which will again achieve something great and make his father even prouder. I can't help but notice the same way his eyes and disposition calm, as though he is thinking of his father and what he's done or how he directs. Whatever his train of thoughts, it's clear he still has dreams in him he hopes to one day realise, and in the future I'm sure he will. As if returning from his mind journey, his eyes look at me again and he says.

"Hopefully I'll get to a stage when I can direct a film, that would really be achieving something, because that's the toughest job ever."

At this point I hear the bustling outside and am reminded of the crowd that has been eagerly seeking their favourite actor's attention all day. While he's been posing for photographs and signing autographs probably since morning, there are still more in the batch who are waiting for the interview to be over so that they can again claim who they have embraced as their own. Stardom is something which leads to fame, and in turn popularity. Whether this is good or bad is debated throughout history as popularity leads to power and gives the individual a false sense of security and highlights them above others. In this field one thing is assured: your stardom may not always be there but while it is it will bring a smile joy to every person who supports you.

Be it the fan, casual supporter or well-wisher, everyone who has met Hrithik today has left with a smile. I ask if actually stops and realises to what extent he as a star touches people's lives be it from making millions smile on screen or meeting the millions off screen, he has the power to make that person who wants to meet him go away feeling better. He again speaks softer than usual, visually humbled by the affection he has received and answers with a sincere tone and a gentle lost look in his eyes.

"I know what I can do and it's something I will never take for granted because it's a blessing. I think I'm really fortunate that I can bring a smile to a person's face just by being there. Which is why I always respect the fact that someone wants my autograph or wants a picture with me, and I always try as much as possible to be there for them and give them the little that they want. Sometimes it becomes impossible to please everyone with the quantity, but as far as possible I do try to please everybody."

Having covered most of the aspects I had intended, yet leaving the treasure chest slightly closed for it to surprise me in our next meeting, I throw a question at him which is completely unrelated to his work and anything he has been asked. This is to be the question that encourages him to take from this interview as much as I have, by remembering of the interviews he gives this one question was totally out of the blue and different and one he had to ponder over. The psychoanalyst in me has been forever dormant (if it even exists), yet I push forward with one of the most bizarre questions I'll probably ask:
If you could be given one of three gifts: the ability to be invisible, the ability to fly or the opportunity to travel back in time to any day and re-live it, which of the three would you choose and why.

Hrithik's eyes focus on me deeply and his lips curl into a smile that broadens and fills his face. He stops the tape recorder and remains silent for a few seconds, still smiling. "I'll have to think about this one," he says as I silently leap with joy accomplishing the final tick on my 'to do' list, brandishing a smile with the knowledge that the answer will be unique.

A few moments later without uttering a word, he turns to me and simply presses record, smiles and begins his answer.
"Being invisible is really exciting, and to be able to fly has always been one of my dreams," he says almost leading me to believe I have my answer.
"But," he continues, "if I could go back in time and live a day," he says before pausing again for a second, building up this answer to it's now anticipated climax.

"I'd really more than anything, more than being invisible or being able to fly, I'd like to re-live the 14th of January, 2000."

I remember the significance of the date and smile, and listen as he continues with a smile.
14th January 2000: the day Kaho Naa Pyaar Hai was released.
"The day that I entered the theatre with the audience, because at that time I didn't know what was happening. I couldn't understand what was happening so I wasn't excited enough. I was more scared than excited.

"I entered the theatre with everybody and some people recognised me and said 'hey you're the actor in the film!' and I was like 'yeah' and they were like 'all the best' and I just said 'thank you'. I entered with them and sat with them. And when the film got over there was a stampede, I was mobbed. They had to call the police force, there was a crowd of thousands outside the theatre and the next show got cancelled and delayed. They could not get me out of the theatre and they had to call guards and pull me out because there were people everywhere."
He looks at me while remembering the day, and repeats slowly "e-v-e-r-y-w-h-e-r-e," his face still wrought with disbelief at the hysteria.

"And I couldn't get out of the place, they had to call people there and put me in a different car and just whisk me away. I was with my friends and I kept asking them 'What's this? What's happening? Is this normal? Does this happen with everybody? What's this?' and we were all stunned and they didn't know what to tell me, they just said 'Yeah this is good, just enjoy yourself!' and I didn't know what to make of it. It was like instant fame. Three hours. That's all it took to change my life. Just three hours. I'd like to live those three hours again. I'd like to feel like the Hrithik before Kaho Naa Pyaar Hai happened and feel like what happened after those three hours, because it's just such a small time frame. My life actually changed in three hours," he says beginning to stammer slightly and wide eyed, still unable to comprehend what actually happened and how it all came about, before the smile returns and he says:

"It's just so amazing! I'd like to go back and live that again, and not only live but observe and actually feel the time change. I want to go back and be more attentive, be able to observe, be able to absorb what was happening, because at the time I couldn't absorb anything."

I give him a few seconds before asking him for a message or something he'd like to relay via this interview as representing or defining him or a period in his life. Aptly he chooses to narrate to me two 'wise men's words', which end our meeting perfectly, symbolising the journey he has travelled and revealing the keys to his attitude, determination and success. He holds the dictaphone close and says:

"There are two sayings I believe, and that I believed in when I was training. The first is: 'The finest steel has to go through the hottest fire'," he says with a sparkle in his eyes, before explaining it's meaning.
"So if you want to be that good, you have to bear the worst thing. You'll make it. And the second is: Life's battles are not always won by the stronger or the faster man, but sooner or later the man who wins is the man who thinks he

can. Positivity and hard work will achieve anything and everything."

On that note we end the interview and Hrithik gets back to his shot, to continue pouring his hard efforts into his work, to please those who have supported him and continue to make his father proud. As we leave the tent all of the extra's eyes are on him, following him and watching their favourite actor's every move. What they see is the image, the character they have seen and fallen in love with as it was projected larger than life on a big screen. What I see is a hardworking actor doing his job and mastering his art, attempting to evaluate what's happened to him and thanking God for every small milestone. What I see is Hrithik Roshan, the man. Someone with the fire of determination in his eyes and a heart bigger than his image. The man who'll win…because he thinks he can.

Fuad Omar

Photo Credit: Subi Samuel

K3G Notes

Kabhi Khushi Kabhie Gham: UK Schedule

Sunday 6th May 2001

It's 0830 on a Sunday morning and Trafalgar Square is occupied and awake earlier than usual. The biting cold weather does little to deter the warm and jovial Karan Johar as he rubs his hands together and looks into a black monitor, before looking at Nikhil Advani and giving the go-ahead to begin. Farah Khan emerges, barely visible under layers of cold-battling gear, but the commanding voice is unmistakable. The sonic boom she usually unleashes which causes feet to blister and sprinkles magic on the ground that shakes as she wants it to, is unusually quiet. Her presence alone reassures me I'm in the right place and her team-up with Karan denotes that the near future will find many of the world's population dancing to her tune. A smile shines from beneath the layers she's wearing as if she's heard my thoughts knowing full well they're true. I spot Hrithik preparing for the shot, his face glowing with a smile which makes me feel as though I'm the only one scowling at the cold. Sporting black leather pants and a cool black pullover with an orange band seeping through, he looks every bit the superstar and is extremely relaxed and alert despite the early hour.

Adjacent to Nelson's Column a team of dancers ready themselves by making sure their costumes are on properly and stand in a line preparing for the shot. The music of Vaande Mataram begins as Hrithik gets into position and begins approaching the camera. The chorus line of delicately decorated girls bearing scarves of the colours from the Indian flag scurry backwards, flowing with the wind that blows his hair back as he smiles and takes a deep breath of British air. The cameraman swoops in and takes his first shot, before Karan analyses the monitor and asks for another take, unhappy with the timing.

Watching Karan's calm demeanour and the spark in his eyes as he scours the monitor, you can vividly see his mind ticking away, picturising a shot or working out the next. Whatever is unfolding in there, you can be sure its result will overflow soon and the quiet, smiling character allows one to glance into the side of him that is brimming with directorial and technical brilliance. The shot is okayed, and preparation for the next one begins. Hrithik comes forward to view the short take and although the difference between the first and second is negligible, it defines the nuances that contribute to his director's midas touch.

Moving on, Nikhil sets up the shot for the infamous Trafalgar Square lions where Hrithik walks forward from behind them and gleams at the sky, his pace in tune with the beat. Some pigeons watch from afar as others attempt to sneak into the area, curious about their new-found friends and craving attention. Watching the monitor, Nikhil sees the near-perfect shot and adds that Hrithik's emergence coinciding with a flock of pigeons flying up would be complementary and so someone is sent to co-ordinate the effect. A re-take later and we are all in splits, as a man whose notion was meant to encourage the pigeons to fly is seen in the top corner of the screen chasing them, causing them to merely walk at a brisker pace, while stealing looks directly at the camera, as if wanting to share in the limelight. The sight of this man shoo-ing them away unsuccessfully and the manner in which they jerk their heads sharply to look at the camera is one to be noted as a classic, and causes smiles all round. A replay later and I have just experienced one of the many memorable moments that are to make up the nurturing of Karan Johar's Kabhi Khushi Kabhie Gham, the project he conceived and is raising much to the delight of an audience that thrives on good cinema.

By 10am we arrive at Leicester Square and Thilaka Paramesh is busy getting her costumes onto the dancers. Her eyes are weary but her enthusiasm unscathed, clothes are nothing short of a passion for this young lady and especially for such a patriotic song which she is humming already. An injection of hot coffee later and the location begins to take shape with cameras being set up, tape being put up around the monitor and a bevvy of dancers being brought out.
As the girls rehearse in their Indian outfits, brightly adorning rainbow colours, a small crowd forms to see why Indian cinema is the only medium truly deserved of the title 'the peacock screen'. The cameras begin to click as the Indian look conjures its cosmic rays, basking onto every face that passes by making it smile.

Once the girls have perfected their steps Farah calls Hrithik who strolls past them, mimics their Bharat Natyam dance steps in unison to the now familiar Indian tune that flows through their bodies, and smiles before taking a bow as they cheer him off. The shot is canned in about four takes and Karan, remaining the embodiment of calm, watches the monitor closely asking for retakes on shots which are canned with too much black in the background or a camera angle which could be improved on. He calls for a re-take after another near-perfect shot, asking Hrithik not to look up as he leaves the edge of the frame, and once more the street of Leicester Square is transformed into a stage of Indian talent and feeling. This time Hrithik does a little jig effortlessly, leaving the girls breathless and exploding with cheer without finding the need to act. As he walks out of the frame, their hearts flutter and they catch their breath, beaming at the shot just completed, and it becomes evident just how much Hrithik loves with a vengeance the field he's in. Giving his all to each shot, he smiles at those around him before and after each take, but only after seeking the seal of approval for the framed sequence by his director. Critical of his own performance, he constantly dashes to the monitor to see the result which got the 'done' tick on Karan's 'to do' list for the film.

The cameras are shifted to across the way, at the park opposite as a street entertainer awakes to capture the attention of the ready-made crowd the shooting has generated. Mr Yash Johar makes an appearance, after silently watching his son hard at work from a distance and he too is positively glowing. In these moments it is difficult to distinguish between Yash Johar - the producer of the movie, and the father whose pride in his son and his artistry is clearly evident in his every look. Karan may not notice it as he readies the next shot, but Mr Johar is quietly watching, blessing every one his son's shots.

Hrithik walks down the Square's park as Vaande Mataram plays again, this time allowing him to sport his brown shades while coolly walking in and out of a clear cut shot which is okayed in a single take. A man dressed as a town crier walks past the suitably situated stone statue of Charlie Chaplin and a few of the unit members' eyes light up like firecrackers in sequence as the same idea pops into their heads. A few run after the Lord Mayor's official town crier and before the smiles are allowed to wither, the magic of the movie seeps through the rugged British exterior of the elderly gentleman as he happily agrees to hop next to Hrithik while announcing his joy with the bell. Farah counts them into the song and another shot is swiftly canned in two takes and the montage is beginning to come together and effervesce with the Karan Johar feel that echoes in one's mind after experiencing his work. The feel-good factor is sprinkled in small doses (literally) as two small tots sit in their prams as the music plays on and Hrithik's face pops in between them to bring sunshine to their day. He mimics a child easily as their eyes remain fixated on him for the split second it takes him to evoke the resounding joy on their faces, their eyes following him with pure curiosity and surprise. Two more takes are shot with slightly different mannerisms and you are reminded why you fell in love with Karan's first venture in a shot which exudes cheer.

The final shot before lunch and two elderly ladies are sat on a bench eating ice cream under the slowly emerging sun, with Hrithik in the middle enjoying his pick of the flavours again pulling faces which magnify the mood of the song, and the feel of the shot, resulting in a joyous way to reel in the first break of the day.

The soft-spoken director steals a smile from behind the monitor, as Nikhil claps his hands announcing lunch, and the equipment is shifted and fans descend onto Hrithik for autographs and photographs, all of which he obliges to without a moments pause now that the shot is over. Mr Johar takes a small step forward towards his son and with a look that speaks volumes, smiles as he too walks from the now complete-shot, followed by the rest of the unit.

It's only a few hours into the day and the cold faces are now warm smiles, the weather has been dry and on the unit's side. Karan has barely shot a minute's worth of footage today and in what translates to so little screen time he has succeeded in making everyone who came out today smile. What wonders will he weave with a three-hour opus?

This is just a glimpse of the magic of Karan Johar and the dream that is Kabhi Khushi Kabhie Gham. Making this motion picture isn't simply about making a movie, it's about making smiles along the way.

DAY 2

The location is Mytchett Place in Surrey and the sun beats down devouring the peaches n' cream complexion of the grand residence allowing every dark corner to come alive with bright light. The abode of some of the major characters of Kabhi Khushi Kabhie Gham welcomes warmly with a secluded scenic garden that overflows into Mytchett Lake and will be the stage for the day for the enthusiastic crew who've the task of making a home out of a purpose built residence.

The film's director Karan Johar is explaining to Kareena Kapoor, Ramona Singh and Jeeru how to perform a scene, and whereas he has previously claimed not to be an actor one cannot help but shake one's head in disbelief as the man-with-a-mission visually narrates the scene in his head for the benefit of his artistes, encouraging exactly the slightly exaggerated cheerful mannerisms he wants to portray. Like a chameleon he appears in many guises, jumping from expression to expression, from a perfect succinct Urdu diction to an accented English twang as he provides the visual he sees inside him and slowly pours it into the eyes of each of his actresses, so their conviction is unmistakable.

A shot is being readied: Kareena in a flash pink number accompanied by a beige skirt walks from the house and adjusts her jacket before fixing her shoe as she approaches a car and its two inhabitants. Resembling fashion's latest victim, she is dolled up in a glam-slam look while maintaining the simplicity of the essence that Kareena exudes. She strides forward with a dainty walk to meet her two decoratively placed friends and greets them as they exchange some ultra-cool linguistic banter as you'd expect from the ex-Beverly hills crowd at a reunion at the local shopping centre. The steadicam follows her as if it is her shadow and finds comfort in her presence.

In a hysterically adept manner she seeming effortlessly completes the scene exposing us to the comical side of the character she plays, displaying how be it Nazneen's (*Refugee*) soft sensitivity or this character's pop-cultured composure, Kareena is master of her forte, which is not bound by genre, only by art.

"Am I looking fat?"
"FAT!"
"P-H-A-T – Pretty Hot and Tempting!"

The shot is okayed after a few re-takes which serve purpose by minor adjustments, but each time the lights are on and Kareena does her thing, she misses the huge smiles and cracks of laughter she's generating behind the monitor which displays her antics as they will be seen on screen.

After the shot she casually walks up to the laughers and sits to see the shot replay, and cannot help but smile herself. If only she could see the millions of smiles she will be evoking in a matter of months when the movie is released. Karan steals a smile too knowing this small but funny scene has got its seal of approval, judging by the unit's response to each take. The clever language he's used, the camera angles he's selected and the way he's chosen to dress Kareena and her chums all collide to explain exactly why this sensitive genius has his finger firmly on the pulse of today's audience, perhaps without even knowing it.

Kareena's shot is over for the while and she pops inside to change out of the attire into a simple soft pink top which reflects the weather and compliments her skin. Next up as if in complete contrast to the outrageous loud glamour look, Kajol appears in purple sari and prepares for her shot by calling Karan. Again from the entrance of the stately home, a shot is canned with Kajol, a British actress and a junior artiste, in a scene which is rib-tickling to say the least. Everyone marvels at how Kajol can repeat the scene without breaking into peals of laughter as everyone around her hide their smiles. Her lips fire responses to the conversation being shot like tornadoes which explode with the very spontaneity that defines the enthusiastic actress.

A few re-takes are shot, each one delivered effortlessly by the two actresses and before you can say 'cut' the scene is complete.

The English actress who also has achieved fame via BBC's Teletubbies later confesses:
"It's quite fun working on an Indian film, it's such a different experience." Dressed up poshly and perfectly composed she can't hide her smile as she reveals, "I recognise some of the actors because I live near Brick Lane so it's a little exciting," before I inform her that after this movie she'll be a minor celebrity in the Asian dominated part of London she calls home.

Mr and Mrs Johar arrive and greet everyone warmly, watching some of the morning's already canned shots. Karan becomes the son in their presence, seeing they are looked after and they in return smile reassuringly at their pride, before settling down to talk.

As the camera and crew are shifted further back from the house, a wide shot of the outdoor is taken and the camera soaks up Mytchett Place's glory. Shortly after the shot and as if on cue, Shahrukh Khan arrives and gets ready for his shot which is to occur within minutes. Aryan receives as warm a welcome as his father, with baby Suhana smiling to all and sundry despite being more intrigued by the picturesque locale she's been brought to. Her goos and gaas reflect her excitement and using her extremely expressive eyes she commands to be taken on a royal walk on the grass, aided by her mother so that she can actually travel while standing. Just like her father, she steals the hearts of everyone present with just a glance and a smile, unaware of the magic she conjures on those around her.

Karan briefs Shahrukh on the scene which features him with Kajol and Hrithik, and he listens attentively absorbing his every word. As the lead pair go through their lines everyone stops to witness an acting class in the institutions that are these two stalwarts of Indian cinema. If there's anyone who can match Shahrukh's spontaneity it's Kajol and if there's an actor who can match histrionics in perfect tune with Kajol's, it's Shahrukh. As the two prepare for battle in a verbal sparring session, exchanging dialogues as though they co-exist with their usual conversation, it seems the whole world stands still and silent, watching them with wondrous delight.

Shahrukh and Kajol complement each other to the hilt, and before the shot people are ready to applaud the mini rehearsal delivered through Karan going through the two artistes lines with extreme confidence in the lines he has penned, and he is gifting to these two reservoirs of talent.

Hrithik is spotted singing constantly between shots. He joyfully renders any tune that comes to mind, while dressed in a tight white top and jeans that make him look like an action figure, much to the delight of toy-makers everywhere. He is not required to do much in the scene, but listens carefully to his two seniors practising, his eyes reflecting the respect he holds for them and the look on his face struck with the same awe that much of today's youth have when they see him.

Before the shot Karan reclines once again to behind the monitor, but as he casually strolls to the screen looking relaxed but never stopping the mind machine which is constantly matching the mental picture with the one he is visualising. His deft direction is certainly in the realm of wizardry, with a clear vision where he knows his characters and scenes inside out.

The scene is meticulously shot and soon over and another simple shot of two of the characters driving away is quickly canned. Everyone is on their toes and relaxed while enthusiastic about how the shoot is going.

Associate Director Nikhil Advani announces lunch as a sequence involving junior artistes is prepared. He too is having a good day with the sun still shining brightly and shots being canned smoother than the charm with which Aryan winks cheekily. Karan quietly moves to look at the set of costumes for the after-lunch shots and the junior artistes are led to be dressed.

For all those reading expecting what the media is promising of K3G I present this notice based on what I have so far seen shot of the movie:

The media are not making this movie and so cannot deliver on any promises, yet are happy to escalate film fans' expectations without having seen a shot of the movie. The man who is making this movie is doing so with his heart and all he's promising to do is to re-create his vision on screen and for the duration of the film bring you into a world he has created and have characters he has imagined tell a story to touch your heart. If what I've seen is anything to go by, leave your expectations at home and just know you'll soon be watching a Karan Johar movie. By the time you've seen this celluloid creation you'll remember why the name alone spells a unique style of filmmaking

and how much you've longed to sit as he storytells once
more.

Fuad Omar

The final version which appeared in print:

KABHI KHUSHI KABHIE GHAM UK SCHEDULE 2001
On the Sets

This week I bring to a close my behind the scenes look at the film that has made history in one week alone and touched a million hearts in the space of three hours and twenty seven minutes. Reading through my diaries has brought memories flooding back and there's so much more that I've only selected certain pieces to publish. I remember the day they shot the opening sequence cricket match in Stowe, and the night of the Screen Awards in January when I visited the sets in Film City. It was a night shoot and Farah Khan was choreographing portions of the Yeh Ladka Haiy Allah song with Kajol and Simone Singh in the amazing set that was Chandini Chowk. I'll never forget walking onto that set, the kindness of the talented team behind K3G and seeing the extent Mr Yash Johar had gone to taking care of his staff that he even got rooms made for them at Film City. K3G for me has been a memorable experience of watching one of the greatest films of Indian cinema come to life, and I will always treasure the UK schedule for its many funny happenings that went on behind the scenes, the hysteria the cast caused and everything that the film embodies. It truly was an experience that reflected what the film is all about: Family.

Special thanks to Karan Johar, Mr Yash Johar and Nikhil Advani, as well as the entire cast and crew of K3G for the memories, kindness and laughter.

May 2001

The sets are of Karan Johar's mega movie Kabhi Khushi Kabhie Gham and the location is Oxford's Blenheim Palace. The shot being framed is between Hrithik Roshan and Kareena Kapoor, and the weather is as bright as the two young stars who are ready to set the screen ablaze in an inferno of freshness and chemistry not seen since yesteryear.

Hrithik is dressed in a white bodywarmer jacket, laced with bright fluorescent streaks and blue denims, Kareena is dressed in white too. A small crowd gather to watch as Karan's saucer-like eyes stare deep into the monitor and he silently mouths the dialogues with his artistes, slowly allowing a smile to escape his lips as he cans the shot he is after. The shot is okayed and another is set up which requires Kareena, her two friends Ramona Sunavala and Jeru, as well as some junior artistes, before Hrithik is required to make an entry. (I can now reveal this is the infamous prom selection scene, and the shot which ends with Kareena asking "So, who wants to go to the prom with me?"). Setting up the shot by getting the extras to perform so they enter and leave the frame rather than yo-yo in and out of it is proving difficult with each take. As some members of the unit go to encourage them to walk forward and not as if they are two way traffic, Karan describes where he wants this shot's principle characters to stand. Associate Director Nikhil Advani goes to have a word with some of the extras who are more interested in being in the frame as many times as possible rather than act as normal college kids, and gets them to remember where they are. A rehearsal later and we all witness why Kareena is by far the brightest and most exciting new actress on the horizon.

Her career may be only two films old at the time of this shoot, but be it carrying off a simple burkha, soft coloured salwar kameezes or bright exuberant items as observed in Mujhe Kucch Kehna Hai, her look is chameleon-like and she slots into the simple and the bold both with ease. This time she's all dolled up to suit her character who in this scene sports a leopard print top and bottom, elaborately decorated to make it look stylish and expressing the nature of her character. The rehearsal has Karan inexplicably describing the scene and explaining each frame he wants to capture with a passion on fire such that you can only nod your head as you catch the flickers and sparks of the flames which dance before you, narrating the scene as it will appear. Kareena fixes her brown eyes on him, absorbing each expression and mannerism so subtly you'd be forgiven for thinking she wasn't paying attention. Moments later your prediction will be laid to rest. Karan asks his heroine to go through another rehearsal and on his command she effortlessly transforms into her character, turning in a split second into a great mimicry artiste who manages to replicate her director's performance, while adding a cocktail twist to it making it her own. Writer Niranjan Iyengar smiles at her performance, as do AD Nikhil and the junior artistes surrounding her. Silently exchanging approving glances, it's unanimously announced the right time to take.

Stepping behind the monitor is always a rush. A scene unfolds before you and one is spoilt for choice as to stare into the coloured digibits which will be magnified to a 70mm or watch the director's reaction or the live scene itself. As the camera pans across the extras and leads to Ramona and Jeru for a 'prom selection' scene, the shot is repeated again and again due to the timing of Kareena's entrance which is not in unison with the framing. Ironically the scene being canned is one where the young Kapoor displays her grasp of timing by executing a comic scene with razor sharp precision and is let down only by her entry which seems to be arriving earlier than scheduled. Many have noted how difficult comedy is because of its need for awareness of everything in the shot and a split second of mistiming and the funny turns into the flat. Yet the acting is not the problem, it's the spatial awareness of the frame and timing of entry. What surprises me most is the ease at which on hearing 'action' Kareena is able to hone into the character's personality and allow it to explode on screen, and then immediately after look in Karan's direction with a look seeking an approval as though she has no idea what she's just done. Acting is not like Thames Valley Water which you can turn on and off like a tap, allowing it to flow in whatever bursts you want, but somehow Kareena manages to accomplish this through harnessing her acting ability like a pro. She manages to deliver on 'action' and become herself on 'cut'. You have to be here to know the spontaneity I'm talking about.

The young girl's talent will probably be allocated to her infamous genetic heritage, but not once has she proclaimed any mileage through announcing her identity. Like a true actress she's let her work do the shouting and judging by today's shooting and the one and a half films of hers I've seen it speaks volumes. Of the newcomers flooding onto the cinema scene, she has the most potential because she is seeking creative satisfaction and definitely is rich in talent. You can compliment her on her looks, but in this industry they will only get her so far. The reservoir of surprises which make each of her shots brimmed with unexpected spontaneity will leave the viewer agasp and assures a Best

Actress award in the future. Mark my words, you read it here first. This one is one to watch.

Karan is delighted with her performance in each shot but the framing and timing of her entry into it agitates him, and given his desire to seek perfection in translating his vision onto celluloid, he keeps re-taking the shot until he has what he wants. My concentration is swayed by the un-seasonary outburst of a merry melody. No, it's not a song thrown in for good measure before the camera but the renditions being verbally exchanged behind the camera as Nikhil and Hrithik are seated adjacent to each other, jaunting out yesteryears' golden hits from even the most obscurest of movies. A discussion on Khel Khel Mein follows, the classic Rishi Kapoor-Neetu Singh thriller and I join in talking about my favourite bits of the film.

Soon enough it's Hrithik's turn to face the lens and dressed in a tight white top he towers over Kareena pushing the frame to its peak. She makes a comment on his presence and he responds with a remark that does not betray his cool exterior, before walking out of the frame spurring off a response from Kareena and her friends which ends the shot with another smile.

As the two stars are whisked away and Karan wraps up a few final shots of the junior artistes, he breathes a sigh of relief. The sun is still shining and time is on his side. Before we know it the day is over and another insight has been served into the making of Kabhi Khushi Kabhie Gham and a few more glimpses are given of tomorrow's talent today. The team have had a gruelling schedule and the small scenes canned today will make up so little of what will feature on screen, but as the UK shoot reaches a climax one can't help but smile taking with one's self the ocean of memories that are full of songs, early mornings and happy faces, and the moments that have made up Kabhi Khushi Kabhie Gham.

Fuad Omar

KABHI KHUSHI KABHIE GHAM: THE BOOK LAUNCH

Kabhi Khushi Kabhie Gham is undoubtedly one of the biggest films of Indian cinema, and the film is accompanied by a behind-the-scenes 'Making of' book written by veteran journalist Niranjan Iyengar. On Sunday 9th December there was a book launch for one of the most anticipated texts in recent times, held at the Grand Maratha hotel in Andheri East, Mumbai. I had the pleasure of attending what was a glitzy evening full of pride and smiles. Read on for the lowdown…

When I received my invite to the book launch it finally sunk in that Niranjan, a good friend, superb writer and fellow journalist, had finally done it and come out with his first book. The invites were small pocket sized replications of the book cover, which opened to say 'Don't Judge a Book by it's Cover', and then instructing the invitee where to be and when. An aptly teasing invitation to what is a very good book's launch, that covers in depth and in interesting detail the making of the most talked-about film of recent times.

The Grand Maratha is a relatively new hotel in Mumbai, but there was no trouble finding it given it's towering presence and brightly lit fountain as I arrived at the gates. I was early and found many of the team who have made the magical experience that is Kabhi Khushi Kabhie Gham bustling around trying to get the set up right and absolutely precise at breakneck speed. In the lobby, I spot the film's associate director Nikhil Advani, dressed in an orange jacket, a tee and denims, casually walking around with his trademark forlorn look, but seeming surprisingly less stressed than usual. I throw a smile his way and he shakes his head, following with the baritone bellow of "Fuaaaad! What's up dude!" making me realise things must be going to plan for the brilliant taskmaster who is as passionate about perfection on celluloid as he is in events, because I've caught him in a rare light mood. I joke about his outfit and ask when he'll get ready to which he cracks a witty retort, and disappears to dress, leaving me to be devoured by those trying to register who has and has not arrived.

Nikhil Advani was a prominent presence in the making of Kuch Kuch Hota Hai, Mohabbatein and Kabhi Khushi Kabhie Gham, and having seen him at work on the sets I am proud to say his growth in his field over the past few years is staggering. He is working towards his directorial debut sometime next year and given his methodical approach to filmmaking, his keen eye for detail and ability to translate a vision to reality, coupled with his understanding of the medium that is cinema, he is without a doubt a filmmaker to watch for. But tonight, he's busy making sure everything goes perfectly.

The lobby is like a museum hosting huge pictures from the film, lit from the ground up, and inside the main hall the colour scheme is as it is on the hoardings – a dignified red and black, with tables laid out as far as the eye can see, a podium at the centre front and a screen to the left.

As guests saunter in, I spot Ayesha Monani, who has clicked the pictures from behind the scenes of the film and has provided the visual delights of the book. She's dressed casual and greets me with a warm hug, before divulging she's in no way prepared to go on stage and has had a nerve wracking journey to the hotel with people constantly asking her what she's going to say on stage…that too when she wasn't even expecting to go on stage. Her pictures are truly slices of moments that made the film but aren't up on the big screen to see, and so the clamour for her work is understandably fanatical. Moments later, Karan Johar, the whizkid director who has successfully stolen hearts time and again through his visions on celluloid, appears in a light lilac coloured formal jacket and white shirt, beaming at the many familiar faces that surround him. His father Yash Johar, a thorough gentleman, greets everyone in his own unique way. Myself with a handshake, co-screenplay writer Sheena Parikh with a graceful namaste and Ayesha with a bear hug that succeeds in calming her nerves some. He has been the resilient support during every filmmaking moment of his son's film and tonight he's no less. Niranjan walks out in a black jacket, trousers and a blue shirt looking the smartest I have ever seen him. Quite a difference from the woolly hats and overbearing coats that draped his shivering soul in the cold mornings of the London shoots. He is extremely happy and greets everyone with a smile and a 'thanks for coming', trying not to appear nervous. As he meets the many outside I venture in with Ayesha and meet his proud parents inside, who are full of pride in their son and his achievements, talking of how they are so happy on this joyous occasion. His mother's eyes sparkle as she speaks, with floodgates of tears glistening in the dimmed light, waiting to flow when resistance gives way.

Around 8pm everyone is inside and the ceremony begins with Karan showing everyone a glimpse of his film and then inviting Niranjan to the stage. Niranjan speaks with an emotional tinge in his voice, unable to fathom this is his day, and gives a heart warming speech that tells how happy he is to have been given the opportunity to write this book and how proud he is of the result.

"The biggest challenge of this book was to try to bring together and represent all the interactions, the scenes, the emotions and technical processes that had gone on during the filmmaking process. What I really wanted to do was to try and show the way Karan thinks and bring across what is going on in his mind, and I hope when you read the book you feel you know a little more about Karan Johar than when you started," he said.

A brief Q and A session followed when the two spoke of the book and it's purpose. Summing things up neatly when asked if his every film would now be accompanied by a book, Karan replied:

"I don't think every film warrants a book, but this one did. Simply because of it's star cast and that so many generations were coming together on celluloid, the fact that Mr and Mrs Bachchan were returning as an on-screen couple after eighteen years, the fact that this will probably be one of the last pairings of Shah Rukh and Kajol, the romantic couple of the nineties on celluloid again, the fact that Hrithik and Kareena were sharing the same creative space as such a huge cast, I think all these moments deserved to be in the book. Kabhi Khushi Kabhie Gham is a film that has a lot of material that deserves to be archived and that is why I feel it warrants a book like this."

An audio-visual followed which showed moments of filmmaking in motion side-by-side with their book incarnation, then from behind a cloud of smoke and the backdrop that was the now familiar family of the film stepped out from the picture frame: Amitabh Bachchan, Jaya Bachchan, Shah Rukh Khan, Hrithik Roshan and Kareena Kapoor, dressed in the familiar red and black outfits that don the hoardings and promotional material.

Karan came on stage and lost in the midst of smoke while being shot at with photographers' flashes said: "This is my family of Kabhi Khushi Kabhie Gham who need no introduction. I now call upon my parents to bring the first copy of the book and hand it over to the head of our cast, Mr Bachchan and release the book officially today."

Yash and Hiroo Johar walked gracefully on stage and presented the book to Amitabh, who opened it, as Niranjan stood beside the family, eagerly awaiting this moment, his family clapping from their table with as much energy as possible, their faces lit with pride at their son's first book release, embellishing the very core essence of Kabhi Khushi Kabhie Gham, which is all about loving and pleasing your parents.

The cast then spoke on the book and the making of the film, headed by Amitabh Bachchan who began by thanking Yash and Karan Johar for the film and expressed his joy during the shooting of this movie, going on to say:
"I have my own apprehensions about the film and really am concerned about my well-being. In this film I turn out Mr Shah Rukh Khan from my house, I get annoyed with my wife Jaya, I consider Kajol to be an outcast, I don't talk at all to Kareena and worst of all I actually give Hrithik a whack on his face! I don't know what'll happen to me after the release of this film, but hopefully you'll all take care of that," he said to a rapturous applause and peals of laughter.

Jaya then said: "Everyone asks me why I did a film when there are so many stars in it, what would I have to do in it? I'm going to answer this question now so please don't keep asking me. First of all I cannot say no to Karan, and secondly when the story was narrated to me I felt that if after Sholay for the first time such a big film is being made, I should be a part of it."

Shah Rukh Khan followed with: "I'd like to thank Karan and his family who are for me my real family, as well as the on-screen family too, even though I was thrown out of their house. It was pleasurable to work with each and every one in this film. Kareena, who I'm sure no one would want as a saali, and least of all me, after having done 'sexy' Asoka with her, and Hrithik, who is marvellous. He's the only one who looks good even without all this smoke! And then there's of course Kajol, a wonderful actress and dear friend, who couldn't make it here today because she's not well."

Hrithik was signed for Kabhi Khushi… before Kaho Naa Pyaar Hai happened and he became a star. Karan said a few brief words at how proud he was of Hrithik and his work and how hardworking he was, leading Hrithik to say about the film:
"I can't express how great it feels to be part of this film and experience. I remember when I was a child and dreamt of being an actor, and tonight I'm standing on the same platform as greats such as Mr Bachchan and Mr Shah Rukh Khan, who are legends in their own right - it really doesn't get any better than this. I thank Yash Uncle and Karan for making my dream come true."

Kareena's introduction fits both her on-screen character as well as her off-screen persona, as Karan enthused:
"She's the entertainment of my film, she's mad and completely cracked but what to do, we all love her dearly and I know I can't do without her. Kareena Kapoor who plays Pooja and becomes 'Poo' in the film."

Kareena dressed in red smiled as she looked emotionally towards Niranjan and said:
"Firstly I'd like to congratulate my dear friend Niranjan who I've known since I was nine years old, I'm truly happy for you Niranjan! I then want to thank Karan for casting me in this film, Yash Uncle for being the wonderful producer he is and I am really proud to be a part of the family that is Kabhi Khushi Kabhie Gham."

Karan then thanked everyone for coming and Niranjan stood proudly absorbing the night he had his first book released. Dinner was then served and in dashed Karisma Kapoor, a long-standing friend of Niranjan with her mother rushing through the crowd trying to find the person she had come to congratulate. Dressed in white she made her way to him and gave him a tight hug exclaiming how happy she was for her friend, who was as surprised to see her and overjoyed.

The evening went on as Niranjan mingled with all who came and was a beacon of light, glowing every time someone congratulated him. Ayesha attempted to stay out of the limelight but as soon as someone recognised her she too was bombarded with compliments. Karan spoke about his film and gave his film's making and Niranjan's first book a breathtaking launch lacking in no department. As I left the Grand Maratha for another appointment, I couldn't help but turn back and smile because I could feel the happiness on the writer's face as his first book was published, and on everyone associated with the film's pride in the product that was launched today. And now there's even more reason to celebrate: The Making of Kabhi Khushi Kabhie Gham has sold out on advance orders alone and is already in its second printing.

The book is available at all good bookshops, published by India Book House Ltd, ISBN no: 8175083387 and priced £20.

Fuad Omar

FILM REVIEW: KABHI KHUSHI KABHIE GHAM

Kabhi Khushi Kabhie Gham is a breathtaking rollercoaster ride of emotion, comedy and drama woven beautifully together through the threads of binding relationships, that endure time, space, joy and sadness.

The film begins with a brief word from the two principle patriarchal characters of Yash and Nandini Raichand (Amitabh and Jaya Bachchan) on the importance of expressing a parent's love for their child, which aptly sets the tone for what's to come. The viewer is thrown immediately into the world of the Raichands as we learn of their family situation and of how their adopted son Rahul (Shah Rukh Khan) is no longer with the family due to a fallout, which comes as hard and fast as it hits their younger son, Rohan (Hrithik Roshan). This allows for a flashback recount of the story which leads to the current circumstances and etches out clearly each character and their relation to one other, as well as the roles defined within the family and expectations that rise from them. This takes the film into the interval, after which the crux of the narrative is how the family are reunited, and what repercussions the split in the family has had.

From its first to last frame Kabhi Khushi Kabhie Gham is a masterpiece. It has every ingredient that has made Indian cinema so great embedded within it, rhythmically progressing the movie through its core strength in narrative that is based in relationships and the family. Karan Johar has not just made a film, he has created a cult populist modern text rooted in tradition that will be used as a yardstick to measure good cinema by. Whereas previously a cluster of films displaying great cinematic technique, sharp screenplay execution, masterful direction, presentation and storytelling have been referred to as examples of how good cinema can be, Kabhi Khushi Kabhie Gham will now sit adjacent to some of these (and precede others) as a dictionary that defines complete filmmaking.

His homage to modern classic cinema is one that pays respect, stirs memories and ensures it too will spawn tributes as he tips his hat to the works of Sooraj Barjatya, Yash Chopra and others, even raking up nuances of his own previous characters' as inside giggle-raisers.

The background score of the movie flows in unison with the heartbeat of the audience, escalating with grandeur as their breaths quicken, and stealing slices of silence when the anguish is numbingly quiet. Even the colour scheme of the movie is in complete tune with the film's soul, with one particular sequence highlighting to the hilt Karan's artistic imagery, shuffling between a bright and colourful song vibrant with life and a hollow, empty resonating echo in a mother's eye as she hears and feels, but cannot see her son. Cinematic experiences don't come any better. The lavish scale of the film is such that every penny spent is seen on screen and the beautiful cinematography captures the locales of Egypt and London in a groundbreaking manner, without causing distraction from the flow of the film. The camera uses a frame rate and pace that cuts like a knife one moment and is slowed down to savouring speed the next, revealing one other technique that Karan has successfully used to his advantage to be able to puppet the strings of his audience's heart.

Performance wise the film belongs not to one actor or actress but to the ensemble cast that is the family. Each artiste has managed to master their role to such a degree that you have to remind yourself that this is a film and you are not watching a real family, and also that you may have even seen some of these faces before. Shah Rukh excels in what is possibly the most difficult role to assay in the film. His histrionics during the scene when we literally feel his heart break for both disappointing the man he idolizes and also because he realises he cannot be with the love of his life is possibly his most violent, because he massacres the viewer emotions in a swift sequence that will not leave a dry eye in the house. His performance is par excellence and to pick out which are the best for any of the actors is too arduous a task. Amitabh Bachchan gives his finest performance in recent times. His presence not only commands respect but for the three hours twenty seven minutes of the film he becomes the father who wants the best for his family, is clutching onto tradition while attempting to maintain control and authority without allowing even his gaze to be questioned. Every viewer will see shades of their own parents in Yash and Nandini Raichand, and will be able to understand, even if they do not agree with, their every decision.

Kajol is a lit firecracker in the entire film that makes bangs and wallops in bursts that light up the heart and screen with no warning. Her screen antics are such that in a one-woman-act she'll make you howl with laughter and dance with joy one second and bring you to tears with a single look the next. It is without a shadow of doubt I can say this is her finest performance to date and one that will be etched in viewer's hearts forever. Kareena Kapoor will have you in stitches by the loudness and classiness of her British-raised character, allowing her to showcase her comedic brilliance for the first time fully. Her sweet yet exaggerated Pooja shrieks for rescuing but ends up forcing you to pledge allegiance to her character that will change the lingo of the moment for a while to come, as well as give birth to a new icon among the college crowds. Hrithik Roshan sizzles in an all-round performance that gives him scope to stir emotions, simply be cool, and play a doting brother and son like never before. His dance moves in You Are My Soniya are electrifying to his and Farah Khan's credit and his chemistry with Kareena is teasingly and explosively volatile.

Song picturisations are a dream in themselves. Be it the spiritual ethos of Suraj Hua Maddham or the playful Yeh Ladka Hai Allah each song in itself is a visual delight. Amitabh Bachchan looks fantastic in his song Shaava Shaava and dances on air with a bevvy of beauties in another perfectly framed moment on celluloid.

Director Karan Johar and Assistant Director Nikhil Advani have woven together a journey of emotions, technical brilliance and mesmerizing screen moments that will live in the audience's memory for years to come. Each scene has so much detail that on repeat viewing one can find the definition of each character and ambience of every location from the framing and background alone, such is the attention to minute details.

Overall Kabhi Khushi Kabhie Gham is without a doubt the most enthralling, entertaining, emotional and complete vision and definition of Indian cinema I have ever seen. It is simply the perfect Hindi film that will appeal to anyone and everyone, and will hold special place in the hearts of the Asians in the UK and overseas who will relate wholly with the boy who brings home a girl to his family immediately edging away from their expectations, the cracks in the family that will haunt and taunt until they are once more enjoined and intertwined and the father-son relationship that has been captured in volumes like never before on 70mm.

This film proves we are not always in control of our emotions…because Karan Johar is controlling them everytime he steps behind the camera. Just as life is a complete experience full of sadness and joy, the aptly titled film completes Indian cinema and rewrites the book of filmmaking. Kabhi Khushi Kabhie Gham is a film you cannot miss, and Karan Johar is a man you cannot ignore, because legends can never be ignored.

Fuad Omar

The New Breed

The 80s was a bad time for Indian cinema. No new storylines, films that ran based on a star's presence and formulaic scrips that did well because times were bad. Salim Khan had temporarily retired from writing and we were left with half-baked wannabes who attempted to no avail to bask in the credibility he had finally brought to writers. The 90s were slightly better and cinema saw things changing again and heading in a positive direction. What does the future hold? It all lies in the hands of the new brat pack of filmmakers who are all set to take on tomorrow, the new breed. Here's a few to watch for and look forward to.

Nikhil Advani is not a name you may have heard of, but chances are you've already seen sparks of his work. Working closely as an Associate Director on superhit films such as Kuch Kuch Hota, Mohabbatein and Kabhi Khushi Kabhie Gham, Nikhil has learnt from the best and absorbed so much from cinema that holding him back any more from his own vision would be a crime. A brilliant technician who works on the sets of any film as though it's his own, Nikhil is meticulous in his approach, dissection and execution of any scene he's asked to contribute to. The man knows cinema too. An avid fan of international films be they from France, Britain or Hollywood, this director has studied cinema to the minutest detail and knows his trolley shots to his jimmy jibs and is a boiling pot waiting to explode. Counting Kubrick films, The Godfather and the work of Woody Allen among his favourites Nikhil Advani is all set to make his directorial debut in 2002. His first film is shrouded in mystery with some reporting it to be a nail-biting thriller and others a love story, but the man who shouts on the sets is as tight lipped when speaking about his film, and is not about to reveal anything. Either way, Nikhil is one to watch and given his reservoir of knowledge about film and passion for good cinema, it's taken for granted any project he decides to start with will be talked about for a long while. Remember his name, he cannot be ignored.

Rohan Sippy. A quiet man whose mind seems to be constantly ticking. When he looks at you, you don't know if he's looking through you or analysing your every move, making a mental note of your mannerisms for a future reference. Those before him gave cinema its greatest and only true spaghetti western and made icons out of Amitabh and Dharmendra with Sholay, but he's not one to rest on laurels that he hasn't earned. He discusses cinema with a smile and seems most comfortable at work on his debut film which is being readied for an August release. With lilting easy going music by Shankar Ehsaan Loy, Kuch Naa Kaho stars Abhishek Bachchan and Aishwarya Rai in a tale that promises to be different and is being finished with no creative stone unturned. He lives up to his film's name and is silent when asked about his first film, wanting for now his work to speak for itself or at least, the interest that surrounds it. Displaying an extreme lack of naivety that accompanies some new directors, Rohan is not someone you'd think is making his first film. Born in front of cinema and knowing nothing else, his thoughtful and careful attitude to filmmaking is just one of the reasons to keep a close eye on him in the near future.

Farhan Akhtar's Dil Chahta Hai came and made a mark in no time. Be it his shooting techniques that blended a trademark Hollywood style of filmmaking, using swift camerawork that took you on a journey and made room for as few cuts as possible, or his ability to successfully define a generation on celluloid, he has definitely made people sit up and notice. The son of noted lyricist Javed Akhtar is already being hailed as a pioneer of tomorrow. His daringly different approach to conventional cinema and the backing of acclaimed dignitaries (with Aamir doing so few films in a year, he chose Farhan's directorial debut as one he definitely wanted to sign on the dotted line for) and a penchant for creating aesthetically pleasing films, Farhan is someone who in little time has raised many expectations. Dil Chahta Hai excelled in music, performance and delivery winning nominations at award functions alongside stalwarts of the industry, and deservedly so. An announcement of his next film is expected soon and the world waits with bated breath.

Meghna Gulzar's Filhaal sizzled with the international audience and got an overall mixed response in India. The sensitivity was there, the pastel coloured world she had created with characters that could be taken from our own town and a story that was very reality based made her an instant hit with moviegoers everywhere. Some criticised her narrative flow and screenplay, while others assassinated her sets, but no one ignored her and with a large portion of the audience she connected. Ask many UK and US cinegoers their favourite film of recent times and they'll cite her debut venture without hesitation. The pirated VCDs of her movie came out days before the film officially released in the cinemas and with the official DVD release having just received a bumper response, it's clear to see she has a lot of people who are backing her. Meghna is a sensitive director who successfully brought new locations, different picturisations, a succinct story and powerful performances together to create Filhaal. Her attention to detail and desire to get exactly the vision she has in her head onto celluloid is her strength and whereas she may not have charmed the crowds back home yet, she's got more than one feather in her cap on a global scale.

E Nivas is one of the youngest filmmakers around and at just 23, his Shool won him the coveted National Award. His film was hailed by some as brilliant and criticised by others as being too dark and disturbing as he brought Manoj Bajpai's character to life in the tale of an honest cop who would sacrifice himself and his family for his cause. Shool marked the maturing of Raveena Tandon for many and came as a wake up call to those who had been coasting along on average cinema for a while. Taking his critics head on, his next venture fast became one of the most anticipated comedies of the year and Love ke Liye Kuch bhi Karega gave the world Aslam Bhai, a tapori Aftab and an ensemble cast performing at their wacky best in a film loosely based on Ruthless People. If he ripped your guts out with his first film, he tickled your ribs with his second. E Nivas proudly hails from the Ram Gopal Verma camp and has learnt fast. His next venture is the eagerly awaited Dum which stars Vivek Oberoi as a policeman who's a victim of circumstance and finds stability in his leading lady, portrayed by Diya Mirza. Vivek is full of praise for his director, and so is the industry. Almost three films old and not showing any signs of tiring soon, E Nivas is someone who has a claim on cinema, and he's staking his claim with every film.

Karan Johar is only two films old yet he gets mobbed wherever he goes and is recognised whenever he makes trips to London. His films have made not only cinematic history but UK Box Office history too, becoming the highest earners a foreign film has made from the top ten in the UK. Marking his entry with a film fondly remembered for its feelgood factor, Kuch Kuch Hota Hai is nothing short of a phenomenal debut. No stranger to the Indian film industry, Karan played a comical character in Aditya Chopra's Dilwale Dulhania Le Jayenge and has been rooted in fashion for years. Be it costume designing, acting, writing scripts or even picking up awards for Best Dialogue, Karan is a director who has displayed an uncanny understanding of Indian cinema in a short span of time that stretches over only two of his own films. Kabhi Khushi Kabhie Gham made history with its complex characters, brilliant visuals, unique cast, entertainment and international recognition, yet still many try to steal the limelight away from the man who just wants to make movies and make them how he believes. Watch him on the sets and you'll know what genius is, ask him about his favourite movies and you're gone for hours. Some may even say he shouldn't be included in the new breed since he's not all that new, but only two films old and raring to go makes him someone who has and will continue to shape the future of Indian cinema.

Fuad Omar

KARAN JOHAR: MAGIC MAN

Karan Johar is the young man responsible for two of Indian cinema's biggest hits. He's also recognised wherever he goes, gets people coming up to him in the street and talking to him with an air of familiarity and has fast become an adopted relative of the cinema audience. Whether he's tugging at heart strings and stirring nostalgia or showing the world what Indian-ness is all about, he's certainly made his mark in no time. Only two films old, an established costume co-ordinator, scriptwriter and director, Karan has left few stones of cinema unturned. His last film was a phenomenal success internationally and nationally. Making the film and through its release he learnt more than he could ever imagine. A journey with Karan Johar that spans the past few years and leads up to the much awaited DVD release of the ultimate feelgood family movie, Kabhi Khushi Kabhie Gham.

What was it like when you took your first shot?
"I remember being very scared when we took the first shot, we were shooting Le Jaa Le Jaa and it was an easy shot involving Hrithik and Kareena then slowly moving onto Shah Rukh. We started shooting on 16th October and then on the 20th the Bachchans were coming. Having them all on the set for that song was the day I fainted! I was really scared, but after the first day I realised the tremendous amount of support that I had and the vibe between everyone and how I would have a great time shooting the film. After the first schedule I realised everybody was

going to get on superbly with each other and that made a lot of difference. The feelgood vibe with each other reflected in the film. After I saw the song after it was complete I really felt it was good and represented the mood of the film."

Do you feel a sense of cinematic growth since Kuch Kuch Hota Hai?

"With this film I felt an immense of growth as a director since Kuch Kuch Hota Hai, in almost every sense. I felt a sense of technical maturity and confidence with this film, whereas there was a little shakiness with KKHH which was translated as innocence. The rawness and innocence wasn't a part of K3G's directorial aspect and there was definitely a higher sense of maturity. I felt I grew along with the film and now feel I know my job. I know I'm secure and this is the place for me. People won't longer think of me as a flash in a pan because I've proved myself with this film and I like this place a lot and this is where I'm going to stay!"

2001 has been a fabulous year for Indian cinema, how do you look back on the year as one for cinema and one which has taught you a lot with regards to your film?

"As far as cinema in 2001 is concerned it's been a great year. There were talks of the industry going through a slump, but it's a case of reflection of the product. I feel good films equal good box office revenue and bad films flop. We saw successes with Mujhe Kucch Kehna Hai and Gadar early in the year, and Lagaan opened new doors where cinema is concerned. I remember calling Aamir and telling him "All of us attempt to make films, you just made a classic." Dil Chahta Hai was very interesting with a different mood and atmosphere working well with youngsters in the metropolitan cities. I'm also glad my film has contributed to the dying coppers of the industry in the last four months and also generating great box office revenues here and abroad. I'm glad it achieved all it set out to do and I learnt a lot from the film's release. I learnt there are people who love me and there are people who hate me, which is something I never realised. I always thought I was this blue eyed loved boy after KKHH but you realise that people change their attitudes towards you when you achieve a certain level of success. You don't change but the people around you do. It's been a process of learning, contributing and attributing and it's been a great year in that sense."

Sections of the media were intent on taking from your success and bringing you down. Your film, despite creating box office history, wasn't allowed to bask in glory for too long because the media was too busy finding faults in it. What do you feel about the media mud-slinging that went on?

"The more successful you get the more they want to bring you down. It's an occupational hazard. There's so many moments of joy I've experienced in the past two-three years making my movies, so the few moments of gham cannot bring me down. I've achieved two very big commercial successes, my first film because it was from a newcomer got the acclaim and the second people tried to bring it down, but the bottom line is you cannot fight box office figures. Because if you notice Fuad, today all those people are quiet because they don't know what to say. Now they'll go hype some other film and deal with that. I've tried to take all good and bad things in my stride because life is exactly like the title of my film: it's khushi and gham."

Although the audience acceptance was achieved, you weren't allowed to enjoy it, did it affect you?
"I feel a certain level of acceptance. We live in our own little world and there's so much more out there we don't really get into contact with. That's why I make it a point to read every mail I get, when I come to London people come up to me on the road and say the most beautiful things to me, and I think back and say to myself, 'Why was I upset with one stupid man who wrote one stupid thing about my film?' There are hundreds of smiles and hundreds of beautiful things I've heard and that's God's way of telling me that this is your audience and it's acceptance. If I can make so many families across the world happy, isn't that an achievement in itself? So why should I let one critic's cynical attitude and attitude towards cinema bring me down? The most important thing to a filmmaker is audience support and that I know I have."

You share a special bond with London, tell me about that.
"The vibe of London just inspires me. I love the place and the weather, when it's dull and grey and raining, and the occasional sun when it comes out. Being in London makes me very happy, I think when I land at Heathrow it just puts a smile on my face. I don't know exactly what it is about the place, it's just I can never feel low or depressed in London. Somehow it has a tendency of making me want to just go out there and have a great time. I genuinely feel good there and when you feel good you think good and you make good films."

Did you draw from any real life experiences for any of the relationships assayed on screen in Kabhi Khushi Kabhie Gham or were they entirely the work of fiction?

"Every filmmaker draws from his own experiences and observations when making a film. A lot of me and my father might be there in a dramatised form on screen. I definitely think the lack of communication is an aspect that I've met within the film that I do go through with my father as most fathers and sons go through. There's a tendency of feeling a lot and not expressing it, and that aspect I have borrowed from my own relationship with my father. But overall there's a basic goodness I get from my parents that during my upbringing they've imbibed and therefore I've emulated and hence produced on screen. I've gained a lot from them like the values they've taught me which I've depicted in my own way on film. That's why the parent-child relationship has come across so naturally because there's so much I've observed and made more cinematic and dramatic, things like I stopped saying 'I love you' to my father when I went from being a boy to man. Why did I stop expressing my love for him? Why do we suddenly become so conscious of hugging them and kissing them in the way we used to, why do we do that? I also tried to develop a screenplay around those questions I've asked. There's a lot of me in the film and everyone because ultimately we all go through the same thing."

If your film is to relay one message, what do you want it to be?

"I hope people take the message of the film home with them that if you love your parents tell them. Because one day it may be too late and you might miss out on saying it and the most common complaint I've heard from people who have lost their parents is 'I didn't even get to tell him how much I loved him' or 'I didn't even get to tell her I loved her', why do you want to wait for that situation? Go home and tell them."

Indian cinema has such a diverse audience and crosses many divides and classes, how do you as a director make a film that caters to such a universal audience?
"You're right Fuad, we are the only cinema in the world that has such a diverse audience. If you see a French film that's made and caters to an international palette it also is in tune with the sensibilities of the viewers in France. Here you have the Wall St yuppie who's watching your film with his family abroad and you have the man in Bihar for whom you have to spell things out and give him a simplified narrative, and you want this film to work and break those barriers, it's the most difficult thing to do. I wanted K3G to work everywhere – in Bengal, Bihar, UP, in New York, UK, Malaysia, South Africa and today I've achieved that, and it's not easy. I wanted to make you in London smile, a relative in Chandigarh laugh and the same in New York, and it worked. For me it was all about loving my audiences as well and it's difficult to strike the balance and if you look at the graph in the last ten years it's only three or four films that have done that and broken the mould. There's Hum Aapke Hain Koun, Dilwale Dulhania Le Jayenge, Kuch Kuch Hota Hai and Kabhie Khushi Kabhie Gham which are the only four films that have worked everywhere."

Who is your favourite director?
My favourite director was Raj Kapoor and if I ever came face to face with him I'd say please hang on and don't leave us because you're great and have taught us everything we know.

In your opinion, which do you feel from Indian cinema's body of work, is the best directed scene?
(pauses and thinks for a while)
I'm getting flashes of Mehboob Khan and Raj Kapoor and Yash Chopra and all of them, I can tell you moments of brilliance in films but…oh God…I think the whole of Kaagaz ke Phool is brilliantly directed. Every moment of that film is superb, that's the first flash I got when you asked the question, I think the best moments of Indian cinema are from Kaagaz ke Phool.

Your favourite scene:
Kaagaz ke Phool as an entire film and in Kabhi Kabhie there's a scene with all three of them with Shashi Kapoor, Amitji and Rakhi in that room and there's a conversation, I think that's the best written scene. Best direction? (pauses) I think I would give it to Andaaz when the lighter comes on and she says everything to Dilip Kumar, but it's actually Raj Kapoor who's there. I love that moment of Mehboob Khan's film. Another one is in Prem Rog when Rishi Kapoor's taking the thorn out of her foot and she says "Tum bahut zid karne lagey ho," and he looks at her and says "Tumne jo karne chor di," I LOVE that moment! These are glimpses of brilliance that come to mind, but I can't tell you the best.

And from your own work which do you feel is YOUR best directed scene?
"Shah Rukh meets Kajol after six years is my favourite scene of my own film that I've directed. But it's to their credit, I just gave them the mood and the atmosphere and the song and they took over. I can't think of a scene in Kabhi Khushi Kabhie Gham that matches that moment."

When did you realise your calling in life was to be a director?
When I saw Hum Aapke Hain Koun. I'll never forget that. I saw the movie and came home and said I have to make movies, and I have to make them like this. I saw it and I don't think I recovered for months. The moment I saw that film in 1994 I knew I had to make movies. Each moment holds your attention for the entire three hours twenty one minutes, despite it having no story, that each moment is so reminiscent of great filmmakers and the way he brought his own flavour in, the fact that he made a musical in its truest form, the fact that Madhuri was brilliant and the romance was outstanding. I still feel it's my top movie of all-time ever. It's brilliant.

K3G has just come out on DVD, tell us about this version that you've decided to release.
"The DVD contains the film in its truest form with nothing cut and in widescreen format, unlike the pirated version which has twenty minutes or so cut from the film, is trimmed from the edges and so on. This official release is presented to you with the correct sound, in anamorphic widescreen, in digital format and is exactly how I want it to be seen."

Fuad Omar

SHAHRUKH KHAN: JOURNEY TO THE OTHER SIDE

Shahrukh Khan is very tired. His whirlwind tour of the UK has seen him dashing from London to Birmingham, doing interview after interview and talking to all who'll hear about his new film. The press junket can be a black hole that swallows you entirely and spits you out when its devoured you of all your energy, and leaves many suffering from exhaustion. Shahrukh Khan is tired…but from his enthusiasm you could never tell.

When I meet him, I know he's had an early start after a late night, and his day has many more appointments after mine, yet he smiles, greets me warmly and is still talking about his new epic with a burst of life that parallels a newborn.

This is why there is only one Shahrukh Khan. His passion for what he does is unrivalled and his ten year journey in his profession has seen him go from crawling and finding footing in the industry, to walking, running and now flying with a film that is the cinematic event of the year, thanks solely to the man sitting opposite me, and his dedicated team.

I begin by congratulating him on not only the movie Asoka, which is easily one of the best films to grace the big screen in recent times (and I'm not talking of just Indian cinema, but generally), but more so on the scale of promotion for the film. I tell him how proud I feel to see the posters of Asoka at every tube station as I go up the escalators and tend to stare at each one so that people notice and want to see what it is that has piqued my interest so much, in hope that they too may go and see it, and how great it is to see him promoting the film and Indian cinema on national television in programmes such as the Big Breakfast and Film 2001. Overall I congratulate on the promotion of Asoka.

"Actually more than me it's my partners, who are Jai Mehta, who actually set this up, and of course Juhi and Aziz. When we realised we were not getting someone to take this film on and release it at that level, we decided to do it ourselves," he tells me.

The biggest compliment I can give the film's publicity is that it truly has been launched on an unprecedented scale, such that when I asked the man selling the Big Issue at Harrow station what the latest blockbuster was, instead of saying the Julia Roberts-Catherine Zeta Jones starrer America's Sweethearts, he says 'It's that Asian film that's everywhere, A-soka!' I give him a smile as I proudly tell him, 'You must go watch it, it's one of the best films I've seen.'
Asoka is everywhere because its launch is by the same dedicated team that passionately made the film, since Shahrukh's company is releasing the movie itself. A risk yes, but given the product is of such high quality for it not to do well would be a crime.

"There were two reasons for making this film," says Shahrukh, leaning forward slightly.

"One was that a director of Santosh's calibre should be given the kind of exposure he deserves. He's already had that with Terrorist and we thought if he's cast me in a film it should just add on. It's also because of the graciousness and kindness that the South Asian audience has already shown to me in the last ten years in London and America and the rest of the world. So we thought we'd combine the two and then Jai went one step ahead and said let's release this film and show we're proud of our film."

Releasing the movie himself is a big risk, especially overseas. Sony claimed it never was to distribute the movie, even though it clearly had made an announcement earlier on, and have since also dropped out of their distribution deal for Kabhi Khushi Kabhie Gham. Instead of feeling bitter, Shahrukh turns the negative into a positive and says he's happy to be able to give a project so close to his heart the launch it so richly deserves.
"When I say we're proud of our film, what I mean is that there are so many people who are not so enthusiastic about someone else's project and they have no reason to be, because I understand that be it Sony or whoever, the film is not theirs and they don't know what we're making. It's our baby and our child and we wanted to give it the best birthday we could, the best chances in life that are possible, and we do that by ensuring it goes to the best theatres in the country and to the best people," he elaborates.

"The second reason was that it's the gratefulness we (Shahrukh, Juhi Chawla and Aziz Mirza) wanted to show as a team to the people living here, who I personally believe have made me such a huge star. My marketability in India is high because I'm an overseas star and I sell well here, and it's not about selling it's about people loving me.

I see a 13-year old kid who met me eight years ago and now she's a twenty one year old lady and she still loves me, it's so wonderful to see her having a boyfriend now and getting married and she's moved on but kept me with her. So I am what I am mostly because of the love given here by Asians and I want to say thank you, and my way of saying thanks to everyone is to Inshallah try and do nice films which are also commercially viable in the Asian market. Another way to say thanks is to say Fuad has been quoted in an article in Total Film, which is read by people who haven't seen a Hindi film before and now will do because of that article and the one they watch is of high quality like Asoka. I can assure you this is a film you can take your friends to, it has a standard popular Hindi film format in that it has songs, it has dances, emotions, colour, a mother, it has everything, and you can show it to your friends and not feel apologetic. Neither would you have to succumb to their pre-conceived notions that Hindi films are a little silly, or it's a little long. Yes it's long and it's got songs, but just like most Chinese films have Kung Fu, we have songs, it's part of who we are and how our films are made. We're trying to say the same thing as the maker of Snatch or Titanic is trying to say, but our language is a little different."

Shahrukh's point dawns on me like an epiphany. As a film journalist, for me the Holy Grail is reaching the point of acceptance from the movie-going public for Indian cinema that is standard of British films and Hollywood. There is no reason for our cinema to not achieve the recognition it deserves, because if anything the same amount of blood, sweat and tears that go into making a film anywhere goes into Indian cinema, yet for some reason it fails to break through the barrier. Feelgood movies don't come any better than the ones born in Bollywood and where the talent is concerned, our reservoir never runs dry.

"If you can overlook the language, the essence is still the same (In Indian and foreign cinema). The performances are the same and the technique is almost the same too, and Inshallah in a few years we'll catch up there too because of the exposure. If the market increases we'll catch up faster and you can see films from the greatest film-producing nation in the world, the longest surviving film industry to Hollywood."

I rock back in my chair letting out a silent 'eureka', as though Shahrukh has just told me the key to a formula I've been trying to understand for years. The answer he gives is spot on.

"It's all about giving it one look. My request to everyone is, and I'm not saying this because it's my film, we have taken a big chance and spent a lot on publicity and got posters everywhere and all because it's our baby, but it is also so you can take one of your western friends with you to see Asoka. So please see it and I can assure you the next time that western friend is travelling on the tube or sits in a barber shop and sees a magazine that has an article on our industry that wouldn't normally carry its reports, he would turn to the barber and say 'Hey these films are interesting,' and maybe he too can spread the word. And that is the only way we'll make it because we can't afford to make it the way foreign films are made, we don't have that market or that money, and that belief in Asoka is what we've taken a big chance on, so I hope it does well."

Shahrukh pauses for a moment, allowing me to take in the revelation he's just delivered. The key is exposure and

Asoka is definitely a film that is being talked about and promoted everywhere and even covered at all times of day from breakfast time to evening chart shows to late night film reviews, and the reason is because it IS of international standard, and anyone can go and watch the subtitled film and get out from it as much enjoyment as a Hindi film fan.

I tell Shahrukh how the film is a success whatever the outcome, because he has pushed the envelope and pioneered the foray into the international arena with this movie like none before him, but how does he feel it will fare in India, I ask.

"Inshallah it will do well in India as well," he says, but frowns before continuing.

"It is unfortunate Fuad, sometimes people have a very narrow way of looking at things. I have been working for ten years and unfortunately am doing a job which is half commerce and half artistic, as a matter of fact it's fully artistic, it's just that it's weighed on a commercial scale. And because it is weighed like this, people get a very narrow picture of what it is."

I begin to catch on to what he's saying, but before I can comment, he explains himself.

"I have taken chances because I believe art has no form, and you can do anything that you want, as long as it entertains people and they appreciate the effort. One has tried to do the effort many times and it's not the failure of a film at the box office that disturbs you, it's the failure of people recognising the effort. Even my friends who have seen the film and like it also weigh it in a commercial sense saying 'Yeah I don't know if it will do well commercially but it's a beautiful film and you'll get a lot of critical acclaim'. Why are these two things separate entities? To me, a good film is a good film and either the business does or does not happen. I hope Asoka breaks that myth, because it's not important to me to earn the money from the box office because I've already put my last penny on this film, and so has Juhi and if we don't recover it then we'll never be able to produce another film, which is okay, we'll still get by," he says matter-of-factly.

I ask him not to say such things because Asoka is at the very least a huge step forward in Indian cinema and it would be a shame if the team responsible for it were not going to continue bearing the torch. He sighs and says it would be good for it to do well because it would show that good films need to be made.

"I just want to break the myth and say here is a film that collected at the box office as well, and good films deserve a special place and appreciation. I hope people watch the film and applaud the effort."

Not only has Shahrukh's team's efforts been applauded, but the good word has spread like wildfire. Be it the Times, the Guardian or the Independent, the film has got attention and fantastic reviews, and is surely one every Asian will be proud of when they see it. I think Shahrukh's busy schedule means he is not hearing all the claps or feeling all the pat-on-the-backs, and so I smile, knowing when his tour is over and he gets a moment to himself his ears will ring with the echoes of applause, and he'll come to know his efforts have not only been appreciated, but embraced wholeheartedly.

I shift topic and mention how I noticed his character in this film had no shades of any other he has played before. Asoka has the same traits as some of the others like arrogance, but it is different to that of Rahul's in Dil to

Paagal Hai or Raj's in DDLJ. He laughs and narrates to me the reason.

"I thank Santosh and Juhi for that! Juhi told me, 'and you don't do any of your acting, just listen to Santosh and do what he says, and Santosh if he tries to do his same old routine just tell him shut up and make him do it how you want him to!' Santosh also had an innocence running through the characters and I wanted to convey that in every aspect of the film. Asoka was innocently aggressive and innocently pompous and naively violent and child like. I wanted to narrate it like a story."

We laugh as the mental picture of Juhi telling Shahrukh to stop acting like he has in the past is one I'm sure any of her fans can imagine, with her frown and child-like smile and finger pointing at him in a telling-off stance, so reminiscent of their many movies together. As I eye the clock I realise my time is almost up, and I move onto an aspect of Asoka that fascinated me: The journey.

I draw comparisons with Paulo Coelho's book The Alchemist, which is also about a boy on a journey to reach his destination, only to find his travels taught him more than where he was heading. A book that Shahrukh has read, he's quick to respond even testing my memory of the character's names, elaborating on the whole aura surrounded by a journey.

"I think the thing about travelling is an Indian philosophy, but I'm not sure. It's one even my mother used to tell me from a story in the Quran. She used to tell me every night, about a boy who's mother used to put some coins and stitch them into his coat (instead of pockets). Some thieves caught him on his way somewhere and stole his horse and said 'Haven't you got any more money? You've only got this much?' and they went off but the boy called them back and said, 'No I also have this much, here take this as well' giving them the stitched coins and he said he did this because his mother told him not to lie. And he said 'I hope you don't harass people who don't have any more,' and the story has inherent in it that you learn as you travel. Even in modern time they say a traveller is very educated, you travel the world and education comes through."

"So the process of life is very important, and this is what I learnt and have mentioned in the epilogue of the 'Making of' book, is that the process holds more value. The shadow or the shade of the tree is as important as the hole that you fall in. The little hurt that you get is as important as the flower that you smell, because it can end anytime. And when it ends, you need to tell Allah, that I did everything along the way. He is not going to ask you 'did you reach the end?' because there is no end. The end is when He decides. And He wants your life to end in a way that you say, 'hey listen, I don't mind if tomorrow did not come, because I saw the shade and saw the pitfalls, and I enjoyed them.' The process is important. God is not looking for you to reach a place, because that place He is. And He calls you to that place and asks you 'Before reaching Me, what all did you see' because He just wants us to enjoy the journey, similarly the analogy is the process of making the film which should be nice, and not the end result. It's a general philosophy which I believe in and I think Santosh also believes in, as do my partners, Juhi Chawla, Jai Mehta and Aziz Mirza."

My eyes light up as I listen to Shahrukh. Not only does he tell stories when he's paid to, but he does so off-screen as well, and a private audience with him holds much to learn. The story is familiar to me, but hearing him narrate it again brings with it a new meaning and once more signifies the importance of the journey and all that is learnt along the way.

Snapping myself out of being enchanted by his words, I realise our time is almost up, and this time he continues before I can remind him, wanting to finish his analogy fittingly, and relating one of the many memories of London he will be taking back with him.

"When we went to the premiere it was so nice and people were so gracious and kind that please do thank them on my behalf in your article. It was great and Juhi called me up, Aziz called and my wife called up and said 'how was it' (about the premiere), and I said, 'I don't know'. I'm just enjoying the process which is so beautiful. And the process ended for us at that premiere and it has been really marvellous the whole journey of doing this promotion and making and presenting this film and that's what matters, what happens in the end result is not important. I hope and pray God gives me enough strength, courage and resources to do this process again and again."

I say a silent prayer on his behalf too, wishing the same, reiterating that this man has much more to give, and Asoka is only the beginning. It is a film that we can take our non-Asian friends to see and know they'll enjoy it too as much as they would any piece of international cinema. Shahrukh talking about the journey of making and presenting this film brings back memories of being on the sets at one point and makes me thankful to have been able to witness a few of the steps and today, share in his contentment of relishing the journey.

Before I leave, as an afternote he adds, with the trademark smile seeping through:
"And of course like I said at the premiere, we hope the western audience soon wants Arnold Schwarzenegger to start dancing in their films!"

Typical Shahrukh, always wanting people to leave with a smile. Shahrukh Khan is very tired, but looking at him you could never tell. Because he's about to jump higher than ever before and scale new heights of success, making sure along the way he's put Indian cinema well and truly on the international map.

Fuad Omar

FROM THE GENERAL'S OFFICE: RAHUL DEV

"Rahul, Asoka is brilliant!" I scream into the phone after seeing one of its press screenings. Rahul Dev is as ecstatic as I am and is eager to know the response, which has been (by all who've seen it), positive. The tall framed, muscle bound actor who has made a major mark by playing general Bheema in Asoka laughs as he narrates to me how he remembers getting the film.

"I was heading into town and Santosh called me to audition for the part. I went straight there and was fumbling all my lines in rehearsals. When the cameras rolled and I auditioned the boat scene, everything just clicked. Santosh is a god, the character of Bheema is superb and I'm very proud to be associated with this movie," he tells me before we share some more of the movie's magic memories. As I go on and rave about Santosh's work, Shahrukh's, Kareena's and his, we move onto the young boy who is playing a prince in the movie too, Suraj Balaje.

"It was so difficult to do my lines with Suraj who plays the child because he's so good! He's doing an international IMAX film now. He's definitely one to watch," Rahul says enthusiastically. Before we say our goodbyes I ask if he has any plans to work with Santosh again to which he replies, "I am proud to be doing Santosh's next movie as well which is written by his father." As we wrap up our conversation, I begin my write up on my Rahul Dev interview and how I first met the man who has so smoothly slid into the role of an actor.

FLASHBACK

When I first speak to Rahul Dev I know things can only be uphill from then. When someone who's a favourite among the people, has hoardings being stared at by everyone from rickshawallahs to high-class socialites and is a presence no one can ignore, picks up the phone and greets you with a friendly "Hi," you know you have half the battle won. Prior to our conversation I had only met Rahul once and that too in passing at the Daman music launch party, had only seen him in Champion and that too in glimpses, and so in theory I had the upper hand since he had never even heard of me. Rahul Dev, superstar-actor of today who's growth in such a short span of time and conscientiousness and dedication was ensuring he would be crowned the megastar of tomorrow, was kind enough to invite me into his home for an interview.

We begin with the introductions and as I show him my work, he courteously offers me everything from lunch to a snack, but I settle for grapes, knowing full well if I feast I'll be asleep in no time. I ask him to go back to the beginning and tell me how it all started, and recount his rise to meteoric fame.

"I started back seven and a half years ago in November 1993, I was studying to be an engineer in Bangalore and was in my last year of college and had come down for a prep leave to Delhi, as that's where I'm from," he tells me as I notice his towering height over me. Feeling rather short I raise my head a little just so I feel a little taller, while mentally witnessing the story..

"I met this guy called Rohit Khosla at Ghungroos Disco, and he was the premiere fashion designer of this country.

So he just saw me from afar and kind of liked how I looked and came up to me and shook my hand and said 'Hi, my name's Rohit and I make clothes and I'd like to shoot you in a few of my designs'. Now I had no clue as to who he was as I have a middle class background and don't hang around with designers. My father was a commissioner in the police and my mother a principal in a school. I was a cricketer in school and used to play for the Delhi State School boys and won awards in the under 15 and under 19 categories, and so life for me was one dimensional. I knew who Imran Khan was and had huge posters of his up on my walls, I knew who Sunil Gavaskar and Kapil Dev were, but in terms of fashion I didn't know one designer from the next. But my friends knew who he was and said he's big and I thought it'd be fun, so we met up two days later."

His story sounds like it could've happened to anyone, and the conviction in his eyes reassuringly hint at how lucky he feels. He re-lives those days as he continues, his every look dancing around his words s though he still cannot believe how kind God has been to him.

"I did a really bad shoot where I was sweating profusely and had no idea where to look when he said profile or I didn't know the A to Z of cameras or how to look. But the pictures came out looking nothing like me, they were stunning and I was shocked," he says with a smile.

"I was amazed and they were really good shots done by one of our top photographers called Prabhota Dasgupta. It was like destiny. The best designer of the country designs you and the best photographer shoots you and even though you do really badly at the shoot and cannot relate to the lens at all, but the pictures come out good because you have some good bones on your face which God gave you and photograph well," he says modestly.

So the genesis of Rahul Dev the supermodel came from a chance meeting, but how did he become the face everyone recognised?

"Raymonds which is a hundred year old company here that makes clothes, they were looking for a man for their clothing and I got the job because of those photos and I signed a two year contract with them. I then signed a year's contract with a vehicle company called the Tata Sierra which was big in 1994, and their only competition at the time was something like the Maruti 800. So it was a big vehicle launch and all of a sudden I was on billboards and in the centre pages of magazines so I got noticed and people were asking 'who is this guy?'. So I continued doing that until 1997, then Mira Nair offered me a role in her film Kama Sutra. She's based in Delhi and we met but I wasn't sure at that time if I wanted to do films. I was in a double mind because I was an engineer and had worked in a tannery maintaining the machines, and on the side was doing picture modelling or film modelling. Which would mean if Raymonds wanted me I would go and shoot for them for ten days, and take that time off work, then see my pictures appearing for the next year round because they would shoot that much stock for the whole year. So it was something I continued doing my job as it didn't interfere with it too much and then I requested to work in the garment trade side of the tannery, because the side I was in was very physical and dealing with chemicals which are not healthy, and thankfully my boss agreed, so I wanted to really be a leather garment exporter and do modelling on the side."

Rahul digs into some grapes and I am by now captivated by his story, engrossed in the story of someone so simple and well brought up, with cricket dreams and business ideas who made his name walking the ramp of fame. How does one go from being an ordinary person to one of India's most well known faces? How did his transition from modelling to acting happen?

"The press were kind to me and featured me as one of the first four Indian supermodels in Society magazine and as one of the ten most sexiest men of the millennium in the Times of India, and so I made my name because the media were good to me. Mukul Anand got to hear of me and I got a call from his office and Mukul spoke to me and offered me the role of Mas Ghul, the most wanted man in the country, in Dus."

Dus. That brings back a lot of memories. Why? Read on next week…to be continued.

WEEK 2
Dus. An unfulfilled dream. The very mention of the movie brings memories flooding back to me, from the time of its launch, the announcing of cast and the amazing stills I had seen of the movie. I clearly remembered Mukul Anand's offering which was to take the world by storm. Technically if there was someone who could achieve what Dus was to be, it was the late Mukul Anand, and he proved that with whatever footage he has left behind of Dus, the stills he has shot and the book he was to have coinciding with its release. The film which was close to his heart was to star Salman Khan, Sanjay Dutt and Raveena Tandon, would've

been a dream launch for Rahul as he'd play India's most wanted criminal, based on the real deal.

"I found this really interesting as he's a real live guy and I had a showreel of him," he says with a spark of enthusiasm showing obvious excitement at playing the character.

"In 1997 the montage of BBC news even featured him. I used to sit with Mukul and watch the clips of him with the beard and long hair, and I had long hair and grew my beard for 29 days. He was the guy who had bombed the Chiraar-e-Sharif, and went out, and the film was about these two commandos who are out to get this man. It was a great experience because we shot in fantastic locations, and while I was training for the film they put me in Kishore Nimit Kapoor Acting classes, where I made a few friends. I made a friend called Jatin and on the last night of the batch he took my number, and two days later he called and was talking about giving me a film, which I thought was really funny. Here's this guy who's studying to be an actor like me and he is calling me up to offer me a role in a film! Well it turned out he was the son of Sujit Kumar and I got Champion."

The story unfolded before my eyes, as I browse through his collection of photos, and spot one from Dus with Rahul as Mas Ghul, sporting a mean look in his eye which haunts me even as I write this. The role would've been perfect for him, he could've pulled it off, but it was not to be. He continues by telling me how things were happening beyond belief for this young boy who had dreams of the cricket field and ended up in an arena which is watched by millions over the world: the big screen.

"I had signed Dus then but hadn't begun shooting for it and so had signed two films before I began! So I believe it's more destiny than anything else, because in school what I wanted to be more than anything else was a cricketer. I used to spend eight hours during Summer vacation and five hours during normal days playing and training myself to be good at the game."

Destiny has certainly dealt Rahul the right cards and he constantly acknowledges this. He was never prepared for what was coming his way, nor had expected it, but as he reminds me: it's destiny. He narrates how he was never an actor and so had to start from scratch and prove himself, making me feel proud of all he's achieved, and realise how much effort he's poured into attaining the position he's in today.

"I was shy and reserved and so it was very difficult for me to take part in elocution classes when in school, which were compulsory. For example if we were doing the Merchant of Venice and we had five principle characters and there's the court scene where Shylock is demanding his pound of flesh and the others are there, well you'd have these guys who'd come and just stand in court. I'd be one of those guys, and that too only because it was compulsory! So it started out as a compulsory activity rather than a passion but now I really do enjoy it. I think because of my experiences as a model, in that you open up more as a person and interact with more people and travel a lot. Also because I went to an all-boys school and had no access to girls and all of a sudden you start interacting, but I still maintain I can't read women at all!" he laughs. This coming from someone considered a major heartthrob, is certainly reassuring for the rest of us.

"Anyway, coming back to 97, we came back from the first schedule and Mukul passed away and so Dus was shelved, and Champion began. The film took a long time to make, around two years and six months to see the light of day, but I guess it happened for the best and at the right time because it earned me two nominations for the Screen Awards, Best Newcomer and Best Actor in a Villainous Role."

Although Rahul did not win any of the screen awards, he was further nominated at the Filmfare Awards for Best Villain and also won an Aashirwaad Award. The fact that the nominations are there alone prove how serious an impact he's made in such a short time. His menacing presence in Champion and Aashiq are not ones that can go unnoticed. His performance in Asoka is mindblowing and in a supporting role he's surely made a huge impact. He looks like he could be Adonis one moment and should be in a Guy Ritchie movie the next, and actually he should be! He would suit a gangster type role anyday, he just has to look at me menacingly and I'd give up my money, but Rahul is too nice for that. He modestly smiles at where life's taken him and accepts what was meant to be has happened, and thus was created the actor Rahul Dev.

"So I guess it all worked out well, everyone liked what I did in the film and it did okay business. It's because of that film I got Feroz's film which I've signed and Vikram Bhatt's and of course I have Asoka. I auditioned for that role because I really respect Santosh Sivan and consider it an honour to be working with him."

Asoka is Santosh Sivan of Terrorist fame's film. It stars Shahrukh Khan and Kareena Kapoor, and is under Shahrukh's home production banner of Arclightz and Films. Paired with Santosh Sivan's awe inspiring camerawork which took the international market by storm in Dil Se and more recently in Fiza, Asoka is one of the year's most eagerly awaited movies. Rahul speaks about how his character is different from that of his previous two movies.

"The character of Champion is an anti-hero, he's a good guy gone wrong and my role in Aashiq is out and out negative. Champion was a character with shades of grey, Aashiq was totally black. Asoka is totally opposite. Whereas in Champion the guy's mission is to eradicate the child he is sworn against, in Asoka his whole life is to protect the child. Asoka is a period film and I play a warrior general from Kalinga who has a slight romantic angle too, but I can't talk too much about the story else Santosh will kill me!" he tells me months before the movie is released.

After Asoka Rahul has many more films lined up, and they too enable him to show off his acting prowess and are complex, varied roles allowing him a diversity some actors hope of being able to display.

"Other than Asoka I'm doing another movie called Mukt, which is set against a Kashmiri backdrop and tells the story of a Sikh family, where a boy's father has been shot by terrorists and his family move to Bombay and what they experience. It's a very exciting film and a challenging role which I'm looking forward to, and then there's a small role

I'm doing in Sunny's film called Indian, as a special appearance."

Since then Rahul is also doing Santosh Sivan's next movie, which I'm sure will be as great as we've come to expect of him. As I eye the time and realise I'm running late for another interview, I ask him to say something about the roles he's been offered and is playing.
"These roles show a great degree of varying emotions and hopefully it'll show that I'm not here to be a star, I'm here to break into the mould of an actor and do good work. I want to shed my image of a model and recognised as an actor, and I'm not from theatre or TV or even have any acting background, so for me this is all new and I'm working hard and hope I can be appreciated."

Little did Rahul know that after Asoka, no one would even see him as a model-turned actor, but now people are saying, 'That guy's great! What? He does modelling as well?' What he had hoped to achieve has been achieved and given the international Asoka is receiving and the accolades given to each performer, especially the main ones, including Rahul, the future is very bright and I'm sure of his hard work, dedication and mission to become an established actor. He no longer needs to struggle but is still fighting, even though there's no need to. But then again, what would you expect from a general?

Fuad Omar

FILM REVIEW: ASOKA

Asoka is a movie by acclaimed cinematographer and director Santosh Sivan, and it is clearly evident from his latest venture that he is about to change the celluloid world forever. The movie is an epic and the first example of International Indian cinema on a wide scale, bigger canvas and projected through the eye of a master filmmaker.

The film begins with the young Prince Asoka (Shah Rukh Khan) as a boy who watches his father accept Jainism, a peaceful religion that encourages him to toss aside his sword, which has caused much bloodshed. The young boy is intrigued by the weapon and picks up the new toy, masters it and soon learns that with the power of yielding this sword comes a great price. A warrior is born who fights many battles yet it is quickly established that this young man is very much fighting human wars, quenching a thirst for power and balancing this with his love for his family, particularly his mother. His mother renounces her son's violent ways and requests him to undergo the greatest education any person can: a journey.

On his journey as an ordinary traveller, the prince encounters friends and learns to eat peasant food with his trusty horse Pawan, who mirroring an opposite reflection to Asoka's seemingly black heart, is pure white with eyes that steal the heart of anyone who gazes into them. While exploring through a forest he meets the Princess Kaurwaki (Kareena Kapoor), whose eyes mesmerise one moment and warn off invaders in a blink. She is the embodiment of beauty and the prince introduces himself as Pawan to her, only to find there is a price on her head and she, accompanied by General Bheema (Rahul Dev) and young Prince Arya (Suraj Balaji), are on their own journey to make it alive to Kalinga where their destiny awaits them.

The journey of Asoka continues with trials and love, jealousy and betrayal, all making up cornerstones of what Prince Asoka experiences along the way. He falls flawlessly in love with Kaurwaki, and she becomes his soul and purpose of living, but destiny strikes a blow when he is called back to the Kingdom of Magadha where his father insists he lead a battle in Ujjain. He returns to the news of his love's death only to begin a mission born in rage and spread by blood. To reveal the rest of the movie would be taking too much from the audiences' viewing pleasure but the journey for Asoka is far from over.

A story of a traveller's travels, his education that is the journey, the loves and losses and wars and redemption all encompass this 173 minute epic that grips the viewer from the moment the camera pans down onto Asoka, as if indicating it is descending onto a mountain full of riches within, up until the deeply disturbing ending, which leaves the viewer with a ray of hope before the credits flash to announce not the end of the story but the beginning.

Santosh Sivan's camerawork and direction are par excellence, as his unique flash-technique and use of many shots to accentuate a minor detail in a scene all add together to create a cleverly woven story immortalised on film. In some sequences the camera cuts like a sword with flashes of residue left lingering both on screen and in the viewer's mind, yet in others following, he uses less shots and still manages to maintain rhythm. His earlier work has proved his technical finesse and his penchant for stealing slices of nature be it through shooting at twilight or toying with the natural elements, and this time is no exception. In what can only be described as god-like subtle imagery, Santosh makes clear his points through once more reverting to nature as we see blood-soaked blades of grass after war and his lens commanding water ripples in more than a few scenes. Water seems to be a crucial element in this feature as it appears as a pit which is expected to swallow man's weapons of destruction, purify one's hands of the blood of another, be a natural bathing atmosphere for a princess, as well as being a hiding ground from approaching enemies and a dying man's final request in another scene. It symbolises life and death, the battleground and safe haven, and it is to Santosh's credit that once more he has pushed the limits of the frame to the maximum, allowing his spiritual side to overflow from thought to screen in the film's ethereal imagery. A film such as Asoka cannot be appreciated on a single viewing alone as upon initial contact one is simply bombarded with an onslaught of visual delights, spellbinding sounds and a story that emerges from our past but still reaches into the depths of every man's soul.

Performance wise Shah Rukh Khan is the life of the movie. His acting prowess is detailed to the fullest in emotional gut-wrenching scenes, that portray innocence, rage, peace and longing all through his demeanour and eye-language. Asoka's arrogance and clarity of his every action, coupled with the consistent river of flowing energy is evident through the actor's performance which to his credit leaves one finding the line which ends with the character and turns into actor. His dialogue delivery is impeccable and physical performance incredible, highlighted by some of the character's most intricate moves being slowed down by the camera so as one can fully appreciate the beauty of the delicately vicious fight scenes, which are choreographed immaculately. Shah Rukh Khan immerses himself within the character and takes on his every trait with perfection, be it kissing the places his mother slaps him or his royally toned voice that attempts to betray its heritage when he tries to become an ordinary man, there is no side to his performance that can be faulted. Asoka could not only be Shah Rukh's greatest screen incarnation, but also a clear message to international cinema of his screen presence, dedication and mastery of his art.

Kareena Kapoor is a revelation. Her presence in the film is clearly an integral one that greatly contributes to its magic. As the warrior princess who acts as sister and mother figure to Arya, a cautious then enduring lover to Asoka and emerges as someone on her own personal journey, in search of her identity and sense of belonging while juggling her duties, heart and mind in a three ring circus, Kareena gives what is by far her finest performance to date. After her innocent and natural debut in Refugee, she is finally allowed to once more realise her potential and play a character that only she could do justice to. Her look sans make up, except a few lines accentuating her eyes as the window to her soul, is as pure as the princess herself and the image of her going to get milk, fully wrapped except for her eyes is of sheer cinematic delight. Kareena has mastered the art of acting with her whole body in a short span of time and her performance in Asoka proves this. An actress worthy of this international epic is seen innocently taking pleasure from a waterfall's pearls of life, with joy reflected in her eyes, the very same eyes that spit fire in a venomous visual assault moments later and cry with anguish, seek solitude and are at the same time a fortress of strength as the movie progresses. Her performance in Asoka is spellbinding and award-worthy, it is safe to say after Refugee and Kaurwaki in Asoka, (as well as commercial successes in her other films) the actress's name is firmly etched into Indian cinema's books, as one of the finest to grace the screen. One hopes her potential is continually unlocked and her future holds many more performances and films of this calibre.

Rahul Dev as Bheema delivers a sturdy performance that takes the viewer into his mind. The role is small but monumental in the way it is assayed. The general's values, his courage and sole mission to protect his masters while repressing his affections for Kaurwaki all come across in powerful flashes whenever he is on screen. His body language, look and tone of voice all contribute towards what is a natural performance that emits a general's exuberance. After the two main characters in the film, it is this one that will live with the viewer also, as the protector who would lay his life on the line for his cause and sacrifice the truth for what he calculates as good judgement. A soldier through and through, it is again to Santosh Sivan's credit for casting perfection in the form of Rahul Dev.

Of the supporting characters, those worthy of particular mention are Danny Denzongpa, the traveller's balance along the way and consequently friend turned disapproving spectator, the young Prince Arya in Suraj Balaji who performs as a future king to the hilt in his mannerisms, vocal arrogance and commanding physical actions, yet remains a child in his innocence and naivety. Raghuveer Yadav, Johnny Lever and Hrishita Bhatt are also ones to watch for.

The background score by Sandeep Chowta is as much a part of the story as the narration. His eloquently composed tunes orchestrate wars and bounce notes off the emotional mood and heightened sensitivity of each character. Anu Malik's music is pleasant and remains in the ambience of the movie, although the dance song Aa Tayar Hoja seems to jar with the overall period feel.

The scene where Asoka is told his destiny transcends that of an emperor is the heart of the film's message. Who's destiny transcends that of an emperor's? The traveller's when he completes his journey. The closer one gets to realising his destiny, the more that destiny becomes his true reason for being. The ending is a rebirth and spiritual hope, that once again signifies embarking on another journey which will undoubtedly be laced with experiences that will make Asoka into the legend he has become.

It is ironical that a film inspired by history is destined to make history itself by being the first Indian masterpiece to be shown at so many festivals, in so many countries and shown nationwide breaking into mainstream British cinema. It is certainly one of Indian cinema's finest offerings and deserves the attention it is bound to receive, missing out on this homage to true cinematic form would be like missing history. Go see it.

Fuad Omar.

Only
the
dead
have
seen
the
end
of
war
-Plato

ARCLIGHTZ & FILMS
presents
asoka
a santosh sivan picture

MOHABBATEIN INTERVIEWS

Shamita Shetty: Close Encounter

Somewhere in MHADA, Andheri, seven floors up awaits a palace with a king, a queen and two princesses. I had secured my royal invite and headed on my way to interview royalty. The palace is Shamita Shetty's abode, a beautiful apartment flanked with images and statuettes as far as the eye can see, but all in a graceful and simple manner. The Ganesha figures watch over the kingdom, sprinkling on its inhabitants the luck the family has been blessed with.

Mama Shetty greets me as I enter and is more than hospitable for the castle's queen, offering a smile, a drink and conversation. Within minutes dressed in sporty casuals, (but not as much as her previous screen incarnation Ishika), the princess arrives, flashing a dazzling smile my way. After I'm seated and offered another drink, she settles on her throne and thus begins an enchanting encounter. Ladies and gentleman, Shamita Shetty:

I begin by reminding her of Mohabbatein's worldwide success, and in particular its position in the UK Box Office top ten, asking how it feels to be part of such a phenomenon and what it was like being one of the key contributors to the Mohabbatein experience.

"It feels great, I learnt a lot during the making of the film. We went through a course with Barry John and were given a lot of training in every aspect of acting from scenes to songs. It was one big learning experience," she says rolling her eyes back as she reminisces causing her to smile the magical Shetty smile.

"Aditya is great to work with, he's very encouraging and especially with us newcomers he used to really push us and enact every scene so we knew exactly how he wanted it to be performed."

I wonder if she saw any similarities between the headstrong Ishika and herself or was she totally detached from the character she played so expertly in Aditya Chopra's second masterpiece.

"I can relate to Ishika quite a bit. A part of me is like her, I'm not an arrogant brat, but my experiences in school were like hers."

Shamita's entry into films was by default but she was not totally unaware of what she was getting into when she was offered a role in one of her favourite filmmaker's projects. Her elder sister's experiences served an educational purpose for the younger sibling who fast learnt the hectic schedule of life on the sets.

"I was getting a lot of offers but I never really wanted to get into the industry. I was doing my fashion designing and after finishing the course and getting my diploma I was offered this film and role which was perfect. I liked the role as it was something I would be comfortable with because Ishika is young and sporty, so I did it. I pretty much knew what went into making a film because my sister has been here for seven years and I've visited the sets so many times. The number of re-takes and shots didn't bother me because I was prepared for it."

I remember spotting Shamita on the sets of Mohabbatein in Longleat, Wiltshire and one of the sequences shot on that day was in the trademark London weather, which brings us on to her love for London.

"London was REALLY cold and I hate extreme climates, so if there's one thing I remember about that place it's the cold! There was one scene which was my introduction scene where I'm supposed to turn and give this expression and breathe hard with a certain look. I remember it was so cold I could not get it right because the lower half of my body was just so stiff and there was a blower on me for effect so it was really difficult to do and so the end result is what you see on screen done with harsh expressions! If there's one thing I remember about Longleat it's the cold climate and it was horrible!"

She shakes her head and giggles as she remembers those days for a few seconds, before we go on to talk about the media speculation with regards to star relatives appearing on screen and the expectations that come with the package of being Shilpa Shetty's sister.

"Being a sibling is tough because you are always compared, but having said that I think I've escaped lucky in that I have not been compared as much to my sister as I could have been, and I hope this continues!"
Shamita is shorter than her sister, and just as unique. It seems unfair to compare someone who's been in the industry for seven years and gained as much experience with someone who is just one film old and a different person altogether. Yet as is the norm in the Indian film industry, the numbers game is a forever evolving ranking and being a sibling is labeled as one of two things: sibling rivalry or someone very similar. Those expecting any of these will be disappointed, Shamita is carving her own niche.

We talk of a typical day for her now that she's made her entry into films, and she describes how routine has kicked in, so those who ever thought being an actress was a walk in the park should think again:

"I get up at 9 when I'm not shooting and have a healthy breakfast consisting of something like egg whites on toast and some fruit. An hour or two later I'll do a two hour workout, then come home and eat lunch. After that I'll get busy with whatever I'm doing like going out or staying in and working on the computer. If I am shooting I'll try and do my workout early in the morning before I leave and shoot all day and come back. Shooting is usually around a 9am-9pm shoot so it takes a lot out of you."

Shamita must have the energy of the sporty Ishika to be able to do so much in one day, and the image of her dressed in sporty clothes and running shoes pops into my head. On the spur of the moment I ask who's your inspiration?

"Probably my Mom, she's a really strong person and I love the way she deals with situations."

Shamita lives with her parents, her sister, her peccanese dog Champagne and a black cat nicknamed Munna, she chooses her company wisely and throughout my visit to her palace, one thing is clear: the Shettys are a very close-knit and welcoming family, showing graceful hospitality and glowing with warmth.

I can't help but shudder at the manner in which the Indian film press treats its stars, more so after meeting Shamita and her family who certainly do not deserve the onslaught of abuse film stars are usually bombarded with in print due to vindictive motives and vested interests.

The film magazines in India usually betray their name. Their titles range from Movie to Stardust and CineBlitz, implying they deal with the magic which is churned out by the Indian film industry but on the contrary they tend to delve deeper into the stars' lives and usually contain concocted stories and gossip-fuelled rumors, often damaging to any star, and publish vested articles unashamed of their vindictive streak. Shamita has fortunately been spared any wild accusations so far and we hope the Indian filmi press begin to take more responsibility for what they write, realizing if their reach is half of India's people, a rumor can go a long way and cause irreparable damage to any star and publishing such malicious lies is a deviation from talent of any journalistic nature, and simply an example of gross irresponsibility.

"I have no clue why they operate like this. I guess our magazines here are sold with a strong gossip content and I don't know why they do what they do, it's something I ask myself too," she says shaking her head as I send a silent prayer hoping this warm girl is never on the receiving end of what the print industry is capable of.

I remind her of when we first spoke over the phone and there was music blaring out over her voice and I thought she was in rehearsals or shooting for some funky new song, but in actual fact that's just how Shamita likes her music to be played: Loud. Her favourites include pop diva Madonna who she's a big fan of and Celine Dion. Hence the conversation steers to the princess' pastimes and how she likes to unwind when she's not playing sporty girls or working on future ventures.
"I listen to a lot of music, music is like my life. It has to be playing in my room for 24 hours. I've started reading

recently too, I like to read murder mysteries and suspense thrillers, but also I like reading something that is related to health or is informative too," she says as I take another sip of my chilled coke, becoming more at home in the royal surroundings.

What else is the young Shetty doing and in what ventures can we see her again on the big screen I enquire, before the princess replies:

"I'm doing one film which is a Sanjay Dutt-Chandrachur Singh starrer called Mohabbat Ho Gayi Hai Tumse (I've Fallen in Love with You), Mohabbat in the title again. That one starts at the end of the month and my role is very different from my debut one as it's more an Indian one and has a totally emotional subject. There's a lot of scope for performance there and the subject is really nice. Another thing I like is that the film has a debut director Rishi Talwar, and with new directors you know they are going to give it their all because it's their big break. That attracted me to the project as well as the very emotional subject so I took it up. Then there's one more film with Partho Ghosh in which I'm opposite Bikram Saluja, and it also has Manoj Bajpai and Mahima Chaudhary in the film."

I nod my head impressed with the two star studded films she has lined up when she surprises me further by telling me about the third film she has on hand.

"There's also a South film directed by Shankar's assistant called 'Chocolate'…". She stops and looks at my face, followed with a two second silence before we both cannot hold back the smile at the title (obviously touching on a food we both share a passion for).

"And," she continues while I compose myself, still beaming at the name, "it's with Prashant," completing what she was saying, before I make a comment about the next interview with her's angle playing on the title of her South Indian film.

We go on to discuss many things including her fans, the letters she gets and how international cinema is not one she has ruled out as contributing to, so if we're lucky Shamita Shetty could be in the next big Hollywood or British blockbuster. On a final note I ask her to give a message to her international fans and after pausing for a moment and again flashing that dazzling smile and with a sparkle in her eyes, speaks clearly into the dictaphone in her soft voice: "Spread the message of love, that's all. There's just so much hate in the world that I think we all need to spread the message of love!"

The interview ends here and I bask in the kingdom's positivity for a while before leaving the princess to return to her royal duties. She sees me off to the palace doors and thanks me for coming, leaving me with memories of an enchanting encounter and hopefully some of the good luck which resonates in the air of her abode. There is a saying that good things happen to good people, and if this is true Shamita Shetty has a lot of good things coming her way.

Fuad Omar

MORE THAN MEETS THE EYE: UDAY CHOPRA

Vikram Kapoor is a totally flamboyant and happy-go-lucky prankster with a big heart and smile to match. Not surprisingly his alter-ego and of screen incarnation, actor Uday Chopra resembles Vicky very much. Meeting Uday is a pleasure as he welcomes me into his home to discuss the success of Mohabbatein and to gain an insight into the man who brought life to the fun loving youngster who became besotted with his adorable on screen partner Ishika Dhanrajgir.

Dressed in a tee and jeans, Uday is as cool and calm as his Mohabbatein character. Sporting a short stubble and biceps to put wrestlers to shame, he is more than happy to discuss what has become the biggest Hindi UK box office success of the year and the experience that has ensured some love stories live forever.

"It feels great Mohabbatein is such a success," he says as with a smile, "not only because it's my first film but also because it's my own production, I'm really happy it's been so well-received internationally."

I congratulate him on his recent performance at the Screen Videocon Awards where all six newcomers danced on stage to a medley of the blockbuster's hits, and ask how life has changed post-Mohabbatein.

"There's been a gradual change, life does tend to change a little because now that you've shown what you can do people expect you to do as well as that or do even better and also you have expectations from yourself to do better as well. After doing your debut film you have to stand on your own feet and make it so in that way I think there has been a change where work is concerned. Besides that we have gained recognition in the sense that we were newcomers and now after this movie we're being recognised on the street so it feels great!"

I joke with him about how I recognised him from before as if you carefully watch the Making of Dilwale Dulhania Le Jayenge you can catch a glimpse of Kajol applying make-up to Uday, to which he laughs justifying:
"I've been assisting my father since the time of Lamhe up until Dil To Pagal Hai and was even assisting Adi in DDLJ so I think when you're someone's brother you became friendly with the cast and the story behind that section you see Kajol putting make up on me is this: We had been out for a long time in the sun and so I just asked the make-up person to put some on me so I wouldn't get burnt from the sun and Kajol overheard and just started putting make-up on me!"

Dilwale Dulhania Le Jayenge certainly is a film full of debuts with Aditya Chopra's first directorial venture and the public's first glimpse of Karan Johar before Kuch Kuch Hota Hai, I wonder if Uday is in the film too which is fast proving to be a lucky mascot for all those involved in whatever way.
"I'm in the film in a small segment, you know the song Ho Gaya Hai Tujko to Pyar Sajna?" he asks as I hum the song inside my head and cast my mind back to the beautiful visuals of the celluloid masterpiece.

"Well, there's a shot when Kajol is walking in the park and Shahrukh goes past her then holds onto her hand and pulls back his hood revealing it's him, there's one person cycling away in the background and that's me!" he says as we laugh remembering the scene. It seems the film's magic has spread further than to it's viewers and will hopefully be one where people will be searching for Uday in it very soon as he is catapulted to superstardom.

We come back to Mohabbatein and Vicky and how close Uday is to the character, as he reveals how the role was written with him in mind.

"When Adi was writing the role he had me in mind as he wanted someone who was like Vicky a little, and with the kind of flamboyance he had and the exuberance and that fun-loving extrovert it's all close to me, so I guess if people have liked my character that's because it was very easy for me to do those scenes as it was how I would've done those things and what I would've said. Vicky is a little exaggerated as is the case with Hindi cinema but otherwise it's me."

Of course Uday has not been through all his character has and so his acting skills came into play. I ask about what training he had received before Mohabbatein and how he prepared for the role.

"I had taken a 15 day workshop with Mr Anupam Kher and that got my juices flowing and into acting, after that I enrolled in the acting classes run by Kishore Nimit Kapoor where I learnt to open up and to shed my inhibitions. Once we had started Mohabbetin we had a lot of in-house training in that we used to perform scenes and songs and rehearse for hours in front of the camera. Then we did a workshop with Mr Barry John from Delhi which really showed me that to acting there's so much more and that acting can be everything, and on top of that we had classes for make-up and diction and dance classes, so ultimately we had a good one and a half years of solid hard work before we went on with the film," he says reminiscing.

We move onto the real Uday Chopra who I am fast realising is an articulate actor who puts thought into his performances and believes in hard work and being a good person and so to delve deeper into his psyche I ask who he'd say was his inspiration be it a real person or fictitious character, and he surprises me again as he quotes me lines from Ayn Rand's Fountainhead and states:
"I read this book which inspired who I became and the character was Howard Roark. He said things like 'a man should have a purpose and the most pitiful person is a man without a purpose,' and 'ego is the fountainhead of all human progress and selfishness is a virtue if you use it right, it can help get you somewhere'. So these things hit me at the time as I had never thought of life like that. Successful people are like that, like my brother and they are true go-getters so if they want something they get it. And they do it for their own personal satisfaction and nothing else, anything else is a by-product. That is what hit me and I realised that is the person one needs to be to achieve something great. That inspired me."

Stunned by what I'd consider as one of the best quotes I've got in a while, I probe further and ask what he aspires to be, and again his response does not disappoint but is an intriguing view of life.
"I really don't know where I want to go, all I know is that I want to keep going there. I don't want to make plans because I think life is so dynamic and every day you wake

up with a new dream and I want to have all those dreams. I don't want to limit myself and go towards just one dream or direction, I want everything. I just want to keep going and maybe one day I'll get there, or maybe I'll never get there and that's the excitement of life that it's just a journey and you just keep going forward."

"I have one film on the floor which is my own production called Mujhse Dosti Karogi which is directed by Kunal Kohli who used to host the show Chalo Cinema. The film has Hrithik, Kareena and Rani and I'm doing a special appearance in the film. So that'll be out next year, and there have been some other interesting subjects I'm considering but I haven't signed anything as yet."

We go on to discuss everything from his clothes to how he loves London and the cold and his workout regime, as well as the common passions we share such as his favourite places in London like Leicester Square and his passion for movies and appreciation for the cinematic experience. Before we end our conversation I ask him to say something to the many millions of cine-goers who will be reading this and have appreciated his performance in Mohabbatein: "Thank you for liking me in my first film, I have a lot more to do and a lot more to achieve. I want to play many more characters so don't judge me on just my first performance and hopefully you'll enjoy the ride, just go with the flow."

Without betraying his cool exterior he thanks me for a different interview and leaves me with a sense of big things coming his way. Maybe the DDLJ magic will sprinkle some more success on this young newcomer whose sights are set high and heart burning with passion. Uday Chopra leaves me restless to interview him again and has revealed there is so much more to the man who gave life to Vicky Kapoor, and that there is as much depth to this man whose eyes are sparkling with dreams and took me into his world for an afternoon, proving in every sense that some meetings live forever…

Fuad Omar.

BREAKING THE SILENCE: PREETI JHANGIANI

The silent lover, the obedient wife, the mourning widower. These are all roles one would expect an actress to play after years of experience and many films, yet one newcomer dared to attempt the role in her debut film. Her youth is also to her advantage as it boldly states how she could never have brought on screen what she has through any experience, yet effortlessly she waltzed into the hearts of film fans everywhere. The role is that of Kiran and the film Mohabbatein, which broke box office records all across the UK and sped up the DVD charts, and the person is Preeti Jhangiani.

I meet Preeti in her apartment and the bubbly actress is far from the docile and quiet on screen persona she has embedded in everyone's hearts, displaying histrionics of an incredible scale which allowed her to carry off such a complex role in her debut film alone.

"I am glad to have got such an offer in my first film, although I was being offered many films I chose this role and the prestigious YashRaj Films banner for my debut, inspite of there being 6 newcomers, Shahrukh, Amitji and Ash, I knew in no other film would I have people working so hard on my look and would I get such an opportunity to play such a tough role in my first film," she says with a smile before elaborating on how she got the role.

"I just went and I met Adi who had seen some of my modeling work and he said you suit this role perfectly, will you do it! It was just great! He had already seen my earlier work as I did a lot of modeling as well as a video for Rajshri Music which was a big hit called Yeh Hai Prem."

Her on screen character does not seem on the same level as the other two as she is more mature and much more reserved, with such complex shades to a person how would she describe the role of Kiran?
"Kiran is actually the role of an eighteen year old Indian girl who is as normal as anyone, but it's just the circumstances which have made her the way she is, and she's a classical Indian dancer. So when I heard it I said this is the best role! I underwent strict dance training for eight months as the master used to come every morning from 7 to 10 and in the evening we used to go for Western dancing with Farah Khan."

The topic moves on to the making of the movie and how it was shooting in London as we are fortunate to have had the entire cast being in Longleat or some part of the UK at some point during the making of this phenomenon.
"Shooting in London was wonderful, it was a great experience. I'm lucky because I didn't have to wear short clothes and I didn't have that many scenes there compared to the others, so in that way I was quite lucky to escape the cold!" she says before I ask what it was like working with Aditya Chopra.

"Adi is a quiet person who is like a maniac on the sets, he's a very tough taskmaster, but then he got the work out of us and is very sure of what he wants. He'll say something like 'this is my character, you are not the character and you have to be the character'. And I remember he said this is one of the toughest roles so at the time I was doing a lot of South films so he said if you're not going to give me the time don't do this film, because you are not this character and you're going to have to live this character for a whole film, which is going to be a tough job. He just totally convinced me to drop everything and go for the role."

As she speaks my eyes search for anything sharp to cut my hands on, hoping she'll bandage them up so lovingly like she did with Jimmy Shergill on screen, but there are no sharp objects or edges in view and so I just let my imagination run wild as the walls turn white and the room transforms into a hospital bed, and as she is already sitting opposite me I pretend she is bandaging my hands, re-living just one of Adi Chopra's magical sequences from his second masterpiece.

I enquire about as to whether she has been typecast in the Indian look mould or is receiving offers which will be different from Kiran.
"I thankfully haven't been typecast and have just signed eight films and only some are glamorous, so it's worked out well. There's a film with Bobby Deol and Mahesh Manjrekar, then there's another film with Firoz Nadiadwala which has Sunil, Akshay and Aftab, and another with Pehlaj Nihalani with Fardeen Khan and lots more. But these three are the ones I am looking forward to most."

Interweaving between fantasy and reality I ask how close she is to her character and whether she has the Indian-ness of Kiran, or is she a hardcore person with tomorrow's morals. This is where those searching for their real-life

Kiran can smile and be reassured, she can exist as Preeti's response reaffirms.

"I'm not Indian in the way that I'm dress Indian, as I only own about 5 salwars, and I hadn't worn them until my videos, but yes value wise and culture wise I am Indian to the core. I love celebrating our festivals and we do poojas at home and in that way I am very Indian like Kiran," she says as I look own to find my hands wrapped in white imaginary bandages, before I look back up with a smile at the girl who is responsible for this dream.

After Mohabbatein has firmly put Preeti on the map, it must be difficult to do other roles as the danger is usually to be associated with a certain type of character and even if she hasn't been typecast, wouldn't future roles have shades of Kiran and how would she filter through accepting a role?

"The role should be a strong character whether it's an Indian role or Western, because I'm not here for the fame or the money, but simply because I love acting and being in front of the camera and I love the stage. It's something I enjoy doing and that's why I'm doing it, I don't want to do a hundred films or work 30 days a month, I'd rather do 15 days and do a few quality films," she says with a mature view of her career.

Preeti has lined up the choicest of films including Awara Deewana Paagal, starring alongside Aftab Shivdasani and Diya Mirza, where she is looking stunning, as well as Wah Tera Kya Kehna with Govinda.

Before I leave, Preeti has a word of advice or even a wish which has come true for her, and with a smile she bestows those words on me:

"Go for your dreams, don't forget your dreams they will come true."
The words ring through as I go down the lift and look down at my bandaged hands, happy to have had the opportunity to learn a little more about the actress who so softly, so quietly and with just one film stole our hearts.

Fuad Omar

MOHABBATEIN: THE MAGIC RETURNS, FOREVER!

A whistling wind blows the autumn leaves through the air, each one carrying with it a million stories of what it has seen. If each leaf could describe an experience or tell a tale, it would span generations and symbolise all the changes it had

seen, the relationships each one has witnessed and how in whatever manner each leaf was a part of every story.

And with this we are brought under the storytelling magic of Aditya Chopra and his cinematic vision of a man whose life was fuelled by love, a man who ruled with fear and the three love stories which blossomed from within: Mohabbatein.

Bring back any memories? The magical masterpiece that went on to create the celluloid experience that defined last October has finally began it's journey into people's homes. As the film's main song requests: 'Steal me from myself, my love. Embed me somewhere deep within your heart'. The words ring true as the film's release finds its place in every home, stealing its viewers away from

themselves, their busy lives and taking them on a spellbinding journey which enthrals for three and a half hours, ending only to find itself embedded in every viewer's hearts.

Be it the pastel coloured liquor which so intoxicatingly lured each filmgoer to the theatres, and tugged on so many hearts' strings or the haunting background score and mesmerising performances of Shahrukh Khan and Amitabh

Bachchan, no one can forget how, like the leaves of change, Mohabbatein is a part of their lives that will always reflect the time it was released, making it a milestone of a movie in every term.

You are invited to re-live the Mohabbatein magic and bring it into your life forever as the film sees its release on YashRaj films video and DVD, packed with extras to delight any fan. As your breaths dance in unison to the crisp rendition of the violin, a menu appears as leaves are carried by the wind onto the screen, yet it is only after the solo has been played that you are whisked away from those memories and can make a choice. The film's transition onto DVD is spectacular to say the least. With an animated menu system and a whole barrel of extras from deleted scenes, an unseen song and the making of the movie to interviews with Amitabh, Shahrukh and Aishwarya by 'Chalo Cinema' veteran Kunal Kohli, the film delivers exactly what you expect: an experience in home entertainment.

The powerful performances by the two leading actors, the bewitching presence of Aishwarya and the arrival of six fresh newcomers who all display talent bounded only by inspiration add together to make this film the masterpiece it is. Under the expert direction of Aditya Chopra, what unfolds on screen is an intricately woven web providing an in-depth analysis of human relationships and three love stories which are born before your eyes. To say Mohabbatein is a journey is an understatement, it is a lesson in

good cinema. A lesson you learn from each time you allow yourself to watch this movie and realise new depths and nuances on repeat viewing.

Hear the rain, feel the breeze and be inspired. You will never look at autumn leaves the same again.

On the Sets: Dum

Sunday 8th September 2002

NESCO Grounds, Jogeshwari (E).

As I ride the highway that leads me to the empty plot that is transformed into a vicious and menacing den, many thoughts travel through my mind. I'm on my way to meet a friend, someone who is only one film old and exudes confidence, speaks in a commanding voice and stands tall like an unshakeable tree. One look alone has managed to evoke fear into many and he knows just what pitch to use to relax you too. The man will always be a gangster personified to me, because whenever he points at me I imagine I'm staring down the barrel of a gun, because what my next move will be is completely in his control. The man is a chameleon of sorts and has in no time established his credentials. His name is Vivek Oberoi.

As I gain the clearance with the guard at the gates, who now recognises me and approves a simple nod, the driver of my three wheeled vehicle seems confused at where he's taking me. Assuming a Chandu style stance, I sniff and tell him in an attempted authoritative voice "Le jaa aagey aur side mein laga do". The poor guy mutters a yes and quivers awaiting his payment. As I walk into the huge vacant chamber that could well be an empty parking lot I see chains, I see puddles of water and images conjure to my mind of if someone wanted me bumped off, this is an ideal setting. It's eerie, it resonates fear and it's straight out of a Scorcese picture.

"Fuad!" booms the familiar voice as I receive an acknowledging nod and sit myself down. Vivek is dressed in a plastic see-through jacket and whatever clothes he's wearing underneath I can't see because of a bright red light beaming down from above. The rest of the space is dark, dirty and foreboding. A man in a yellow T-shirt grabs me and hugs me: it's the film's director E Niwas, a young filmmaker whose National Award winning work has already gained him credibility and a lifelong pass to Ram Gopal Verma's World of Adventures. "When did you arrive?" he says with a smile and before I know it Vivek has also sneaked up on me. A bear hug later, he explains how they are shooting a song sequence and unless I sit well away from an imaginary line I'll be drenched soon as water will be sprayed onto the dancers from every angle possible. Ever since I met Vivek Oberoi I've liked the man. He's straight forward, knows how to handle himself in the company of the right people and can discuss film intelligently. He also has a warm rugged way about him that either you like or hate. Fortunately we clicked instantly and I've come not to interview him, not to even do this write up, but just to check up on a friend. As the shot is set up, there's Ganesh Hedge, expert choreographer and someone who has an enviable stock of talented dancers behind him going through routine with his boys. These are the chosen ones that grace the stage abroad whenever there are live shows and are used to the screams of the many, but today they're here to be soaked. All clad in black vests and track pants, they assume a regimental position, and Vivek joins them at centre spot up front. Donning dark glasses and a rigid care-a-damn look, he stares into the space in front of him with a momentary 'bring it on' attitude, until Ganesh says 'Now!' and the water begins to spray. From every angle a jet of hard pressure water is being hurled at these people with such force it would probably move an elephant, but these guys stand rooted to the ground. The shot is a crane shot from above and so all we'll see is the streams of water in unison, merging above Vivek and then disappearing over a sea of heads and feet from a top angle view. The shot is taken around five times before Vivek is guided to a seat beside me, dripping wet, a towel over his head and wearing a very tired look.

"We started shooting at 7 this morning and I'm starting to feel unwell," he tells me looking very weary. I tell him how I sympathise given the amount of water he's being sprayed with and how it can't be good for his health. He begins to shiver slightly and a boy dashes forward with a drink and begins removing his shrunken shoes and soaked socks. Vivek puts his head back and ruffles the towel slightly to dry his hair, then looks at me with a sorry look that makes me request director E Niwas to give my friend a break. A smile later, we're all joking around and are pleased to get a few moments in between shots.

"Dum should release around December 6th, that's what we're aiming for," E Niwas tells me. "The music is by Sandeep Chowtha, I know you'll like it." He whistles to someone to start the music and plays me a fast beat funky track from the forthcoming film and tells me I can get my own copy in October when they release the music of the film. Vivek has been messing around with me for the past few weeks since I told him I saw a teaser poster of Dum that shows a blood soaked face of his looking up menacingly with the caption "Can you face him?". I told him the size of the poster and look reminded me of Chandu and sent shivers down my spine. He sent me an sms back saying 'Good, now I can't wait to face you.' Vivek is a young actor who has it in him to make it big. The media will do all they can to satisfy their own intentions and cravings a la recent comparisons with Hrithik, but Vivek has his own game plan and it only involves hard work and concentrating on being a good actor, rather than the media's favourite flavour of the month.

We talk about a few of our favourite films and what we've been up to, recent releases and plan trips to London, and before I know it it's time for the next shot. I've chilled long enough suffering a few mosquito bites (mercifully a small price to pay when compared to what Vivek is enduring) and feel I should make my exit now before I end up missing my next appointment which I cannot be late for. Having moved our chairs from one end of the lot to the other repeatedly to get out of the water's way, we get up for one last time and say our goodbyes as he always does: with a smile, a hug and a genuinely warm adieu. Every time I go to meet Vivek Oberoi I'm reminded of the hard hitting gangster he played and every time I leave I'm left with the memory of the man behind the characters he so easily assays. He gets into the skin of each role be it by spending times in the slums or sitting in on training at a police academy, no one quite brings to a role what Vivek does. But then why am I telling you all this? I just dropped in to see a friend. Give him time and you too will see if you can face him. Dum is scheduled for release in December.

Fuad Omar

The Story of a Princess

'*Aishwarya*' in *Sanskrit* means Wealth and Prosperity. Someone who lives up to her name is Aishwarya Rai.

The ex-Miss World, model and ever-growing actress is a personality who needs no introduction. Nothing less than a fantasy to many men, a role model to women across the world and a beauty who has made her name in the world of modelling and film since the day she stepped behind the curtain of the silver screen.

When she entered the film industry she was greeted with bouquets and compliments and everyone wanted to sign her, but as time went by the interest died down and the press realised they had found a new foundation of controversial banter, and then there was silence. She is not one who plays along with the media game that dangles a carrot in front of her every once in a while, or indulges in PR exercises to highlight what she's doing. She was written about non-stop for months on end recently and not because her films were making box office history, but because of her association with Salman Khan, the other media whipping boy who wouldn't entertain their whims and desires. They couldn't get to him through him so they got to him through her. By writing almost every detail (no matter how fabricated) about the two star's relationship from beatings and bangings to break ups they began an in print assault which threw more assumptions their way than any one could justify. Finally the tirade has stopped and the press are now trying to find something new to write about after lost sales, angry fans and achieving little close to nothing where Salman and Aishwarya are concerned. We read about what apparently she's up to but rarely about the constant attacks she undergoes and the survival, or the quiet resilient fight.

I remember when I first met Aishwarya at some public function I can't even remember the name of, but I can clearly recall the way a room full of people parted to make way for her to walk as well as her leaving a trail of heads behind her who'd follow her every move. She looked a lot more fragile in real life than she does on screen. It was a few years back and my brief conversation with her at the time was something to the effect of "how do you travel so much" and her response was detailing her itinerary for the next few days which would clock up more air miles than Richard Branson. As someone poked there head forward and asked for her autograph, she smiled, nodded her head at the fan and became engulfed in a sea of people.

I remember thinking at the time she would not only be huge soon but also wondering how she copes with the immense pressure of stardom. How did she travel to two places within hours and still manage to look fresh? How could she be so tired from her running around and yet still be able to smile for every camera that wanted to click her. It seemed she was living in a world that demanded (and received) much from her. After she left for some shooting or other commitment and was away from the country the thoughts still haunted me at how she managed to deal with all the attention, and how strong she must be to take what's thrown her way – a physically demanding job that comes with verbal abuse in print from time to time.

I remember seeing Ash first on the UK stage when she came here for the series of concerts with Aamir Khan and Akshaye Khanna around the time of Taal's release and how almost half the people who came to that show had turned up to see Aishwarya as every time she was on stage the darkness of the auditorium would vanish under a sea of clicking and flashing light bulbs that lit up the atmosphere, each one trying to capture a frame of her. The first time she came on stage from underneath a silvery cloud I watched the audience, the second time I watched her. The way her feet would stamp the stage and the smile she'd give the crowd, the way her eyes would dart a quick look at the audience then at her co-star and the energy she embodied, I knew while people were caught up in her magic they wouldn't see half the effort that she had so carefully given each number.

The Ash I've seen is the survivor, putting up with being in every gossip paper and mag every month and being the victim of a scrutinised life. For her, being judged was not over after the Miss World contest and the initial response to her entry into the film world, this was just the beginning.

Aishwarya has been publicly maligned by the Indian and some of the international press, by journalists who if you meet now, will speak highly of her. Although the negativity bows when these people actually meet and talk to her, it still surfaces in print. Those who write against her often change their attitudes but this never comes out in print.

The accusations were many so I'm not going to go through the list or dissect each one but will say after observing her on the sets I can say she's a thorough professional. Despite the rumours of interfering, she does not and just goes about her job, taking time to listen to the director and nod her head while keeping her eyes focussed on who is talking to her.

The way she listened attentively to Adi Chopra on the sets of Mohabbatein, pays close attention to Annes Bazmee on Radhesyham Sitaram and Sanjay Leela Bhansali on the sets of Devdas is not written about.

The smile she gave at Wembley after she finished her piece and the way her eyes scoured the arena in amazement at every face or the way how every time I meet her despite it being few and far between, she always smiles and has never given me reason to believe anything that's written about her. The way she has grown on screen in front of our eyes and gave a once in a lifetime performance in Hum Dil De Chuke Sanam and gave dance a soul in Taal. I honestly didn't think there was much acting scope in Taal for Ash, but in HDDCS (which released almost simultaneously) it ensured no one could ever doubt her talent. She hasn't had the opportunity to showcase what she can do since then, and this is not her fault.

This is what people don't write about.

Films like Hum Dil De Chuke Sanam don't come round every day nor do ones like Sanjay Leela Bhansali's Devdas, where Ash is glowing as much as the sets. I remember marvelling at the sets of the huge palace which was erected and had a lake built around it. The mahal which had arches and polystyrene walls with small mirrors in every corner so at night the moon would reflect off the palace and shine over the lake too to create what is one of the most beautiful things I've ever seen. She's doing her job on the sets and the film looks set to be amazing, given

Sanjay's style and direction with artistes of Shah Rukh, Ash and Madhuri's calibre.

Until then she has films lined up like the old backlogs of Radheshyam Sitaram and Hum Paanchi Ek Dhaal Ki, and will undoubtedly come under more fire by the press. Her presence in Mohabbatein was spiritly to the hilt and her quiet Indian demure was appreciated by many.

Ash is a misfit in the Indian film industry and I say that not because of her talent, but because she doesn't deserve the constant maligning she is forced to go through. Of all the interviews I've read of hers I'd say they only carry 30 percent of worth, because no one has yet been able to get through to her and ask the right questions that bare her soul. Maybe she doesn't want to and that's why she carefully answers what she's asked but doesn't reveal too much.

She's getting through what's being thrown at her and will have wrapped up the backlog soon, and will dazzle the world once more very soon. This article is written to say don't believe all you read about her in the gossip press and all those who have been waiting for her to shine again have only a short time to wait, because as the world holds its breath, the princess is set to reclaim the throne very, very soon.

Fuad Omar.

TOURS

Millennium Masti 2000

Wembley Arena was alive with musical entertainment and 'masti' on Sunday 14th May, as Farhath Hussain's "Millennium Masti" concert hit London in style.

The sixteen-day tour which began in the US, went onto Canada and Spain and finished at Wembley, was a night to remember for Bollywood fans. The live stage show lasted 3 hours and pleased an almost packed auditorium, which resonated with the sounds of whistles, claps and screams as some of the Indian film industry's most popular names dazzled on stage.

The evening began with the hostess Malaika Arora dancing onto stage and telling the crowd how much she had anticipated coming to Wembley. Throughout the evening she lived up to her name which literally means 'Angel', as she sweetened up the crowd before each act, encouraging them to make as much noise as possible.

She introduced the beautiful and sensuous Sonali Bendre who danced to a popular song from her superhit film Hum Saath Saath Hain, before marvelling at the enthusiastic crowd saying throughout the tour she kept asking "When are we going to Wembley?" as she had heard no one could hold the hoards of fans back from supporting their favourite stars.

Saif Ali Khan was introduced next and performed a medley of recent film hit songs to an audience in raptures. He danced enthusiastically to songs of not his films but of other recent blockbusters including Kaho Naa Pyar Hai and Khauf, mimicking the onscreen dances to a hilt, before removing his shirt and throwing it into the audience.

Raveena Tandon, a regular at such stage shows was greeted with equal enthusiasm by the crowd and she danced to various filmi and non filmi pop songs, before Bobby Deol one of Bollywood's heartthrobs came on stage to a thunderous applause. His routine dance and song medley of songs from Gupt, Soldier, Dillagi and Kareeb, ended with a note of thanks to the fans who had come to see him on his first UK stage show, and for the love they had given him and his brother and father, who are both actors.

"It is because of you and your love that I am here," he said as girls screamed his name watching on dreamy-eyed.

The only star who had not yet come on stage was the show's headliner and had his name chanted before Malaika could finish introducing him. The video screens displayed a flurry of images from his various hit films and prepared the crowd for his arrival. Salman Khan, Bollywood's biggest heartthrob walked on stage dressed in a white suit and casually threw his sunglasses into the audience creating a frenzy, as fans clambered to catch them. With an entourage of dancers he danced to songs from his UK box office hit Dulhan Hum Le Jayenge, as well as other songs from Hello Brother, Jab Pyar Kisise Hota Hai to name a few. He received a superstar's reception and said as he looked out at the sea of people:

"I come here every year, year after year, and you always welcome me back. I haven't seen so many people here before, it's because of you all that I am where I am today.

You have a choice, I don't, and I'm very fortunate you chose me."

He then turned around joking saying "I'm not going to face you if you're all going to continue screaming when I'm talking," which only aroused more hysteria.

Salman then rendered in his own voice to the crowd of thousands a song from his forthcoming film "Har Dil Jo Pyar Karega", before telling the audience, "I love you all and will be back on stage soon, enjoy the masti!".

Musical interlude was then provided by two singers who performed two songs from recent films which kept the audience entertained in between stars, before Malaika returned on stage introducing the second part of the show which had many double acts by the stars and even interaction with the people, bringing audience members on stage to dance with the stars. Saif Ali Khan said he was looking for a "Papaji" before selecting a burly Sikh gentleman from the audience and dressed him up in knee pads and sunglasses ready to dance with him, which had the crowd in hysterics.

The second segment was full of many stars on stage and having fun and Saif Ali Khan even surprised with a guitar solo to the audience's delight, with Salman dancing on stage. When he held the microphone to Saif, he just laughed, "I can't play and talk at the same time, man, I'm not that good!"

The evening ended with a bang as the stars came out to thank the crowd with the shows promoters, and Farhath Hussain announced his next show would be in August with stars such as Shahrukh Khan and Sanjay Dutt. Overall the evening was enjoyed by all and the enthusiastic audience ensured the show was one no one would forget.

Promoter Farhath Hussain was overjoyed at the tour's success and said,
 "The tour itself went well with Toronto having a very good turnout, but nothing beat Wembley, it is always the best."
 "The London show was historical and had an amazing turnout and a fantastic crowd".
 He had delivered on his promise to give a show full of fun and worthy of its namesake – Millennium Masti.

Fuad Omar

The following interview was conducted in May 2002 and was one of the most requested for reprinting by fan sites, readers and Shah Rukh fans.

SHAH RUKH KHAN: FROM INDIA WITH LOVE!

Shah Rukh Khan is one of India's biggest superstars and he's coming to London and Manchester's biggest venues this Summer for a live spectacular event that will promote Indian cinema for a worthy cause. Meeting Shah Rukh is always more than a pleasure, it's an experience. Seeing him perform on stage is another experience altogether.

When I meet Shah Rukh, he's lost weight since I last saw him and is looking thin, making me enquire as to whether he's eating properly. "I lost it for Devdas," he tells me as we sit down and spend some time catching up first as he's just got off a plane and walked into a press junket. If he's tired he doesn't show it, but then again with Shah Rukh you can never tell. He's forever the bundle of energy that inspires others and once more he's coming to our shores to sing, dance and shout about his favourite topic: Indian cinema.

India With Love is the biggest Bollywood event to occur in the UK and is set to be an experience of a lifetime. When Shah Rukh came in 1995 with Aamir his concerts were the most-talked about in years and are to this day counted among people's all-time favourites. Two years ago he returned in a visual spectacular which saw him descending onto the stage breathing fire and presenting a self-made parody on the Indian film industry pioneering a live stage theatrical story infused with the songs of his most popular films. He single-handedly brought London to a standstill last year when he came for the premiere of Asoka and has gained fans in everyone from Jonathon Ross to David Fincher, so this time too; it's little surprise his arrival is nothing short of an announcement of a huge event.

"I was sitting in the plane and I read Mr. Bachchan's interview saying it's a great honour to be performing in Hyde Park. For me, I'm used to playing with my son in Hyde Park with the ducks!" he begins as I ask what it's like to be performing in an open-air venue much larger than the ones he's previously graced in this country.

"It hit me that I'll be performing there and it's a very big event in front of so many people, it's a major institution and for a great cause which is the Prince's Trust charity. I was sitting in the plane thinking all this, and also for me it's just like you mentioned, coming and blowing fire all over again!"

"I don't like to differentiate between the audiences of different venues, I just like to come and do things from the heart. I'd like to come and give it my best and just have a great time on stage, yes there will be a language barrier because this show's for both Asians and non-Asians, there's a cultural barrier and a location barrier because we've never performed there, but I don't want to think about it. I just want to concentrate on doing what I do best and giving it my all and I'm sure Mr Bachchan and Aamir feel the same way too."

If there's one man who's been pushing the barrier that holds Indian cinema from the acceptance and appreciation it deserves for a long time and is all set to break it, it's Shah Rukh Khan. He's appeared on almost every mainstream and alternative television show and spoke to so much of the international press explaining the ethos and essence of Indian cinema, converting many along the way to the truth that cinema is cinema, whatever language it's in. He's aware of the show's associations and venue and that it's aimed at a wider audience than just the core Asian fans, and is prepared to once more be part of a pioneering project.

"We will concentrate on doing maybe one or two items in English or speaking more in English which will be the live equivalent to watching a Hindi film with subtitles, and so the other audience don't feel left out but enjoy it as much and take home memories of these five people who came down and sang and jumped around and danced and gave it the best shot they had. And hopefully not only will we take back with us a part of London, but those who see the event will also retain a part of Asian cinema very close to their heart as well."

For as long as he can remember Shah Rukh has looked up to and idolised Amitabh Bachchan. He knew everything about him and even bought the same cologne as him, adopting it as his favourite. When you look up to someone for so long you one day outgrow them as you make your own achievements and conquer your own mountains, but Shah Rukh explains how for him, the man who changed Indian cinema history and is a living legend will always be someone he's proud to look up to.

"If you discount Aishwarya and Preity, I am the most junior of the guys, so I don't think I can come close to Mr Bachchan or Aamir where their achievements are concerned. I've never worked with Aamir in films but know him very closely and have worked with Mr Bachchan in a few films and the desire has always been to just stand there and let him do his stuff and his brightness will let me create a shadow, which in itself is very beautiful. I'm just honoured to be on stage with Mr Bachchan and Aamir and be a part of this and that alone is a very big achievement for me."

"I did a show with Mr Bachchan in New York with Govinda, and was called last minute, flew in and rehearsed something in the afternoon. What came across from working with him was that I used to think I work very passionately and very hard with a lot of attention to detail, but when you work with Mr. Bachchan you realise that he's like a nervous child doing his first show, his first school play every time and that quality is what I feel makes him very endearing. More than the persona or the greatness of his acting or the amazing quality of control that he has, that's the side everyone sees, but more amazing than that is the manner in which every time he mouths a dialogue or walks on stage he's doing it as though it's the first opening of a school play in that rare manner. So I'm going to just go there and react to whatever he's doing which is what I did in Mohabbatein and Kabhi Khushi Kabhie Gham"

The live experience is very much a personal interaction with the audience unlike cinema. Shah Rukh may have been told by certain sections of the press that his Asoka didn't work, but the audience in every cinema internationally said otherwise. When the lights go down and the microphone's on, all that he knows is that thousands of eyes are on him, something very different and more personal than the direct response a film can generate. Asking him about the live experience, I catch the sparkle in Shah Rukh's eye as he enthusiastically reveals the nirvana of being on stage.

"I've always been more of a theatre actor than a film actor, and what we do on stage now is different when theatre was more serious. It's 50 percent like a rock concert. People say you go and dance at weddings and private parties, and my view is that when I come down and perform here it's like a wedding or a celebration too except in New York or London or Australia or wherever. And I know the Asians who have thronged there it is a great moment of pride that someone has come from abroad and is doing what they would love to do in their houses but are unable to because of the pace of life here or the position of life in a Western country away from their homeland. When people are cheering you can feel it, it's as though they're saying 'Whatever you're doing, we're really liking it' and it reminds them of back home, so whenever I do something live, it's about returning that warmth. It's not about how many people there are or how hard they're clapping or how much they've paid, it's about me trying very hard at that point in time in saying 'you've invited me to your party, I'm going to do my best to make sure you go home having had a great, great time and night out'. That's my whole take on shows, it's about having fun and generating happiness. When a show's over, I'm really tired and my knees are hurting and I'm carried off the stage and I wish I could carry on all night, I get that much out of a live show."

Being whisked away with him as he describes the experience, I try to visualise the sea of faces that will all be mesmerised this June and be chanting his name, alongside cheering for their favourite stars who are bringing the magic of India…with love. The magic of the movies is not something that is replaceable and as Shah Rukh goes on to explain, he's hoping he can just introduce a spark of that magic to the audience and relay the warmth that exists on the peacock screen.

"I think magic cannot be recreated, it just happens. You cannot plan it and go into that much detail and say this one show will sum up Indian cinema and say what it's all about. I think already because of people like you, because of the films that are coming here and the curiosity that surrounds our films and the fact that our country is producing the largest number of films in the world, all contributes to the attitude that this cinema can become a part of my life. It's not about a fad or forty-two days of Bollywood, it's about the essence and I hope it does become a part of people's lives. So when you go to Leicester Square and see a film by Quentin Tarantino or Spike Lee, you can see an Indian film also. It will take time and slowly we might get there, but hopefully this show will give them a taste of the warmth of Indian cinema and show how different it is, and they find it very different from a rock concert or anything else they've seen on stage. They'd never expect Al Pacino, Robert DeNiro or George Clooney to come up on stage and start dancing, so they have to be aware of the fact that yes, we have songs in our films and that is why we can do this dual role. If we didn't have songs we wouldn't have what we have in live shows, we could only come and speak and mouth dialogues. It will take a little time for people to understand that a film star of India is not just a film star, he's a rock star, an action and singing star and is all of them rolled into one, he's a walking-talking variety machine. It will take some time for them to understand but I hope we're able to make them aware of the fact that this is how Indian culture and cinema works."

As I'm told that my time is almost up, I thank Shah Rukh
for once more giving me much more than I expected, and
that's the very marvel those coming to the biggest live
Bollywood event can expect: the unexpected. His back-
catalogue lists the best films of recent times and the spark
in his eye hints that this is just the beginning.

"I'm very proud to be a part of some of these films and
very proud that Devdas too now is going to Cannes. It's
great to see good cinema coming down from India and
being appreciated as the faxes and emails reflect and
Inshallah we'll be able to explain Indian cinema better to
them."

You have been warned. Shah Rukh Khan is coming to
town and this time he's a man on a mission.

Fuad Omar

HEARTTHROBS SET THE STAGE ON FIRE

Saturday 22nd June 2002
London Arena, Docklands

When it comes to live stage shows, there are events and there are experiences. Heartthrobs 2002 was definitely a major event that had to be seen to be believed, creating an experience for every member of the audience they will not forget for years to come. The show has been years in the making and longer in anticipation. What began as an eagerly awaited Hrithik Roshan show that sold on his name alone had snowballed into a live event that promised to be the first of its kind. There's only one first time and the entourage of talented young performers who came and gave their all, conquering the UK stage and imagination of their audience, many of them gave performances that reflected a professionalism and perfection that belied a debut.

The show's compere Raageshwari kicked off the masti by pumping blood through to everyone's hearts, getting them racing with enough adrenaline to start a fire. Singing some of her hits including the immensely popular Duniya and Oye Shava, the young, but-now veteran stage princess gave a long-overdue and resoundingly popular UK debut, and having said this before I still believe her place is on the international stage, with no less than the best. The wonderful singer and bubbly Rags needs only a moment to charm her audience and then for life, they're hers!

She humorously introduced a man appearing in rags, after stating Aftab had been in an accident on the way to the arena, allowing him to slowly peel off the mummified bandages and turn to the audience causing hysteria among the young fans who had waited so long for their favourite to come this side of the country. In a sincere performance that was trademark Aftab-to-the-core he ploughed through a medley of his hits such as Deewana Mujhe Kehta Hai, Deewana Mera Hai and Mast, in which he got all corners of the arena to join him in screaming at the top of their lungs, cheering him on further. A visibly moved Aftab dashed off stage to soak in the warm welcome he had just been given. He has been waiting a lifetime to address his fans like this, and he realised tonight he has many more than he ever could imagine.

The lights dimmed and an ocean of beacons began dancing across the back wall of the stage as familiar notes played and an angel in white descended from above. Karisma Kapoor entered to the tune of Fiza and received a rapturous applause that ensured a smile never left her face thereafter. After teasing the audience with this small segment, Arjun Rampal exploded onto the stage to screams and cries as he launched into his hot favourite track Jaan Le Va from the international success Moksha. His first deadly look towards the crowd caused a ripple of arms to wave and try to reach out to the man who has in so-little time become a part of so many's lives as a dream come true. The tall, lean and muscular framed Rampal gave an energetic performance that left many breathless even after he had left the stage. No one was expecting him to move the way he did, poised with grace, an earthy ruggedness and yet still dancing like a pro. When Arjun jumped, his feet stamped the stage while landing in such a way that coincided with the thunderous roar of the now-manic audience. As girls clamoured to the front trying to get closer to their idol, security began pushing the crowd back, all while Arjun coolly smiled and told the audience how happy he was to be there. Realising the magic of the moment, Arjun grabbed a camcorder and told the audience he wanted to savour this forever as he filmed the audience that cheered him on. If he had any doubt of how much of a cult star he has become, it was wiped from his mind instantaneously.

The darling of British Asians everywhere made her first appearance on the show clad exactly how the fans remember her, in the guise of the lovable and fashionable, Oxford-New Bond St-hopping Poo from Kabhi Khushi Kabhie Gham. Earning many catcalls and whistles, Kareena Kapoor made an impact from the moment she walked on stage, the same way she has done so in every frame of her celluloid ventures. Echoes of It's Raining Men caused almost all the female members of the audience to jump up and down and show solidarity in sisterhood with the fashion-conscious and ultra-high brow Poo, and some even mimicked the 'Ooooooooh' that complements her on-screen antics. Kareena is here to stay because she has proved not only can she capture your heart on-screen but steal it on-stage too.

The man who had made miracles happen in the past two years was next. To give him tags and names would never do him justice, just like all phenomenons the only way to know the atmosphere that filled the air when people knew he was next, is simply indescribable. Hrithik Roshan made his London entry in style, dressed in cool black and showing he is the king of stage as well as screen, causing what can only be called beyond mass hysteria as he danced to Ae Mere Dil from his debut superhit film Kaho Na Pyaar Hai. His body flowed with every beat as he executed the most intricate of dance moves, leaving many gaping in awe and realising the magic they had expected to see had been surpassed the minute his feet touched the stage. The crowd roared further as he danced with two toddlers teaching them his infamous jump from the song, giving them a kiss each before they exited stage left. He took the mic to thank everyone and say how he had been looking forward to finally performing in the UK, and introduced a surprise guest of the evening, Salman Khan, who entered waving to his fans who reciprocated with screams untamed. After a few words he introduced his brother Sohail Khan's new movie trailer, before bringing out Sohail himself and requesting the movie-goers give him as much support as they had given him.

A slightly restless audience began feeling the withdrawal symptoms of the live experience but rose to their feet once more as Kareena took centre stage, her body hovering to the music of San Sanana San from Asoka before being surrounded by bandits who were after the warrior princess. Her hero emerged yielding a whip and in a moment generated more screams and mesmerised all as he walked calmly to his princess and stole her heart. Arjun, appearing in a see-through black top and black baggy pants, sporting a tilak on his forehead, gazed deeply into Kareena's eyes causing the audience to melt to the tune of Roshni Se in what must be one of the most romantic and sensual live performances I have ever seen on stage. The manner in which the two artistes carried themselves and co-ordinated perfectly a romantic's dream left many breathless and did justice to the wonderful picturisation of the on-screen version of the song. A beat later they were surrounded and the audience began shaking their shoulders and dancing away along with their favourite twosome to the popular O Re Kaanchi song from Asoka. This was without a doubt one of the many highlights of the show and left a resonating presence with many. Kareena is a joy to watch and the best thing is there's so much more in her and far better things to come, she always succeeds in taking your last breath away. Arjun has proved in these two performances alone that he had stolen the show, the dude who won the Best newcomer award earlier this year, proved once more why exactly he is one of the most exciting things to happen to the silver screen in a long time.

After stealing your hearts and exiting stage right, Arjun paved the way for the jovial Aftab who tickled it with a hilarious performance from Biwi No.1 with Karisma and another dancer. Teasing each one and delivering his usual comic mannerisms, the youngest of the Heartthrobs went from Ruki Ruki to Mirchi in no time, ending his stint by paying homage to the world cup and hurling footballs into an already ecstatic audience. By now it was clear the fans were on a pleasure overload and had gotten much more than they had expected, but the magic was far from over. After a few more songs and a heartstring-tugging performance by Raageshwari, the back lit up with stars setting the stage for Hrithik and Kareena to saunter on to the voice of Jab Dil Mile Mile, which got those who had any remaining energy in their bodies to dash forward and try to get a closer look at their favourite heartthrob and sensation dancing alongside the girl who has brought a new angle on Indian cinema. The song was extremely well choreographed and melted into Mujhe Kucch Kehna Hai's Iss Pyar Ko Mein Kya Naam Doon as everyone's lips mouthed 'ruppa pa ruppapa pa' and the feet began tapping. Those who paused to regain their breath, did so wisely as Hrithik emerged from the front of the crowds to Rind Poshmal with every drumbeat seeing a fan leap forward trying to touch his hand as he reached out to the audience full of smiles and love for those who have put him where he is and helped ensure no amount of bad press can knock him. Every time he appeared on stage, not only was the shrilling response evident, but also the magic he brings with him. People's faces lit up and they began laughing and crying unable to contain the happiness of seeing the young boy who has grown through so many different roles in no time and found a place in the hearts and minds of everyone, deservedly so as he gives back just as much affection he receives. As if this gesture was not enough, the beats of Bhumro began and he emerged after Kareena dancing with ease like a man with an endless well of energy, before disappearing into the dark to claps and screaming compliments, as well as 'I LOVE YOUs' and 'DON'T GOs'.

Light entertainment followed as Raageshwari called a Punjabi sardar from the audience to dance on stage. The slightly overweight and thrilled taxi driver revealed his desire to dance with Karisma and answered all of the compere's questions incorrectly and hilariously, his nervousness of being on stage clear, yet also his impeccable comic timing. After convincing the young host to call someone to dance with him on stage a girl was called from the audience who seemed shy of the burly man at first, until he slipped into something more comfortable to dance in. Peeling off the layers, the audience gasped as from underneath the turban, thick black beard and pregnant belly came a lean, mean Adonis in the form of Arjun

Rampal, who had successfully fooled everyone, leaving the girl on stage covering her mouth as she shook her head in disbelief before attempting to mutter 'I can't believe this' into the mic. The dashing dude took her hand and launched into a Punjabi song and dance, where she moved with him accurately, yet still had plastered on her face a look that defied the logic of what was happening. A hug later, a huge white teddy bear gifted and probably a heart pounding like never before she walked composed off stage, before widening her eyes and screaming as she reached her seat, sharing her thrilling experience with the friends she sat with. Calling more on stage and requesting the overly tight and less-understanding-than-any-sane-person security to relax, Arjun brought two youngsters together and even got them to propose, fall in love and shot his cupid arrow right through their hearts, giving them phones to make sure they'd keep in touch for more than the five minutes following their moments of glory. He then caused a security nightmare by inviting any and every girl to join him on stage for Pyar Ishq aur Mohabbat and this was the moment many of the event security realised: you can't hold back affection, so move out of the way or get trampled on! The bevy of girls who made it to the stage hugged him as he lifted them, touched his hair and danced with him until the lights went out and each one was safely returned to their seat.

It is ironic that in a show called Heartthrobs, Arjun ensured his name, charisma and presence was clearly etched into the hearts of everyone who came to see him. With an energetic aura hovering around him that oozed a magnetism never-before-seen, the young man of steel evoked screams and sighs, stealing not only every young girl's heart, but also their heartbeat.

Karisma and Hrithik appeared together on stage as the excitement continued with them rendering the romantic Chand Sitare from KNPH and causing the women to swoon and the men to hold their partners close, for what turned the auditorium to the liking of a college prom. Lovers swayed to the scintillating music with their gaze fixed on Hrithik and Karisma, both who exuded a chemistry none-expected, sweeping each other off their feet and causing many hearts to return to normal level in a soothing lullaby.

Announcing the next number was dedicated to the man who made everything for him possible, Hrithik paid respects to his father with an unrestrained and heart-warming smile as his eyes scoured the arena welling up slightly not only from joy of the moment he basked in what he had achieved and the many who had come to see him, but also for being his father's son, a man who has inspired him throughout and taught him to be the person he is today. Sitaron Ki Mehfil was probably the most anticipated song of the evening, having already been performed on stage in his debut film the crowd went wild on seeing it before their very eyes. Hrithik moved like lightning, doing every choreographer he has worked with proud and making certain that wherever his father was, he knew he was dancing for him and so he danced straight from his heart to the beat of his soul. Cheers and cries, slogans and screaming reminded everyone in the arena that magic was being made this very moment as heartbeats got faster and a huge round of applause followed his once-in-a-lifetime performance. Visibly emotional, Hrithik caught his breath before saying a silent prayer thanking God for all he has been blessed with, something he does often taking each high as a humble gift. Backstage he was greeted with pats on the back and hugs, returning victorious from a difficult and physically demanding routine that he carried off in a way that seemed effortless.

The show ended with Karisma's lively and entertaining rendition of Hum To Mohabbat Karega which had everyone singing alone, followed by Aftab's huge favourite Dil Pe Chaane Laga from Kya Yehi Pyaar Hai and Arjun's clad-in-black Aankhen. Returning to the stage for one last adieu, Hrithik evoked hysteria once more with You Are My Soniya, where he and Kareena literally recreated the magic of Farah Khan's choreography and Karan Johar's film to the hilt, in what had everyone's heads bopping to the beat. The grand finale followed with the entire Heartthrob cast being reunited for Bole Churiyan where everyone looked amazing sporting similar outfits and danced like a dream, gaining the audience's final remaining drops of sweat and tears, as they sent them off in the warmest possible way, London-style and full of smiles. As with any show, it had its minus points, most of which were due to bad organisation from the UK promoters side, and seating arrangement and pricing meant anyone who paid under £60 for a ticket had a poor view of the event, but these are all covered in my column this week, here I want to just review the show.

Overall the show exceeded expectations, and proved true that you can't set out to make magic, it just gets created when the sparks are there. The six sparks that joined together, catalytically fuelling the other ensured the night was one never to be repeated and committed to be one of those magical evenings you remember with a smile and warmth, feeling content you were a part of it. Hrithik dazzled, Arjun evoked awe, Aftab endeared, Karisma crackled, Kareena mesmerised and Rags refused to let the audience be bored for even a second. In what must have been one of the best live shows to date, the long-awaited Heartthrobs certainly came, saw, entertained and conquered. Disappearing into the night, the sky glowed brighter as returned to it were those it had lent us for one evening only. When it comes to live stage shows, there are events and there are experiences. This one blew them both away: it was sheer unadulterated magic.

Fuad Omar

COMMENTS:

This week saw the Heartthrobs shows kick off and come to London in what has been a chaotic and hectic time. From the moment of landing to the time they left, the Heartthrobs were surrounded by fans, doing publicity for the shows, giving their all and making the most of what was set to be a historic show. Kudos to Hrithik, Aftab, Arjun, Karisma, Kareena and Rags for what they achieved and making the shows go so well given the restrictions of the venues. In this issue you'll read my review of the show and what happened. Here's the unfortunate negative side that hopefully didn't ruin any part of the show for those who attended and saw the event from in front of the stage. First and foremost, the majority of problems during this tour arose from extremely poor organisation from the UK side, so the stars were not always given adequate transport, drivers, security and even food. If an event organiser is unable to cope with or handle a situation, he simply has no right to be holding the event in the first place. Unfortunately after a great run of US shows, the UK leg of the tour was dogged with problems from day one. Whereas the stars were accommodating throughout and just wanted to put on a good show, it is sad for me to say that the London Arena, which is where for the first (and hopefully last) time such a live show was held. The security at the venue were terrible and extremely rude and obnoxious to many attendees be it from the audience or even those performing. They seem to fail on two levels: knowing their job and knowing how to talk decently. Let's hope the organisers realise their mistake and never turn to the London Arena again to host a show.

Secondly the seats there were organised as such (and again in accordance with the seating price plan) that if you paid less than £60 for your ticket, it meant you did not get to enjoy the full experience due to some obstruction or the fact that your seat was too far away from the stage. Next up security again attempted to stop certain portions of the show taking place. They managed to halt some of the pyrotechnical aspects and at one point even attempted to stop Hrithik from climbing up to reach out to fans, almost sabotaging his act. Hats off to the amazing young Roshan for keeping his cool and continuing for the audience's enjoyment without being distracted by idiots who know no sense. In Manchester the show began very two hours late due to (again) bad organisation on the UK side meaning those up north only got some of the complete show. Overall the show went smoothly and all spectators loved what they saw, and the bottom line is the tour was a huge success. If you went to see the show (and emails have already dictated many of you have and loved it) then if you got a great event it was mostly thanks to the stars and performers who gave their all despite having to face difficult conditions, thanks to incompetent organisers. Either way, let's hope lessons are learnt for the future as I'm fast losing all respect for those dis-organisers who do not understand the 'show' aspect of show-business and only want to see the 'business' at whatever expense. Believe me, the heartthrobs and I mean everyone from Hrithik to Aftab and Arjun, Kareena and Karisma and Raageshwari thank all the UK fans for coming out and supporting them, they are touched by your affection and have left extremely charged. Thanks for making the final days of a long world tour very memorable, and know every scream, every cheer and all the placards were appreciated.

PREITY WOMAN

Preity Zinta has zing-a-zing-zinged up the ladder of success in no time. From a very natural and bubbly debut in Dil Se to an inspiring performance in Kya Kehna which signified the Indian film heroine was heading in new directions and could personify a strong positive character and be accepted. She's done the hip, chic roles and even played a brilliant cop, but her new role is probably the most exciting: that of an evolving film actress at a time when change is coming.

Indian cinema is not only moving forward, it's breaking barriers as well as records. Gone are the days when a Hindi film heroine was required just to look good and dance around the hero, she now has a voice and the audience wants to listen. A role model who established a close rapport with her audience almost instantly, Preity Zinta is not only part of the ride that is hoping to break new ground for Indian cinema, she's also a prime choice as an ambassador of the medium and that's why you'll see why she's one of India With Love's most closely guarded secret weapons.

When I speak to the bubbly actress, she's in Cannes soaking in the buzz that resonates throughout the world's greatest film festival and greets me with a chirpy Hi! Ask how she's doing and she draws a deep breath that exhales oodles of energy as she bursts out, "I'm good! Enjoying myself Cannes, lots of things happening!"

The gal's eager to talk about her first ever UK stage show and the opportunity to address her fans, as she can barely contain her enthusiasm.

"I'm extremely excited because this is my first stage show in London and the first time is always the first time, you never get it back," she tells me.

"It's also the first time that Amitabh, Shah Rukh, Aamir, Ash and me are together on one platform doing something and I'm really excited because it's the best from all of us and an experience for me. I'm just waiting to come and see you guys!"

Gathering words in between gasps of breath she smiles and tries to explain how excited she is, and finds there are none. She's just waiting to show the UK how much fun she wants to bring and says:

"I just want it to happen as the energy and enthusiasm is really building and I can't wait for it to begin."

Kundan Shah's Kya Kehna established Preity as a strong and positive role model for women everywhere in a role and film that only comes round once in a while. It also opened doors for actresses everywhere that until now were closed, and made the certain filmmakers and audiences realise that celluloid women too have power and can get a message across without compromising commercial success. I enquire as to how Kya Kehna changed things for film and the identification audiences found with her on-screen character and the bubbly actress who had something to say.

"I think as an educated Indian person who has travelled a lot and has now entered the film industry, it's important that we do films that are educational sometimes as well as entertaining. So I think with Kya Kehna certain things were established that India being the second highest population in the world, we don't talk about certain things and even now in Indian families there is a lot of restriction, for example parents don't discuss sex with children. That film discussed things and appealed to the youth and so I feel in a certain way people do identify with me in the sense that in cinema new things are happening, and we're taking new issues into form that portray the problems of India today. It's this new generation and they identify with a recognition of these problems and the way we discuss it."

Being her debut film, Kya Kehna was no walk in the park. By the time it was ready for release, many were sceptical as to how it would fare and not because of its content but because it had taken so long to make. The outcome proved not only that a fresh subject can stand the test of filmmaking time but also that an effervescing and exciting actress had arrived on the scene. Preity, a newcomer at the time, was oblivious to how effective her performance was while shooting.

"It took forever to make Kya Kehna and was very difficult for me because I'm not a trained actress and have never gone to acting school, so to maintain that consistency was tough. At that time I didn't feel it was acting because in roles like that and so early in your career you're new and you're just 'being' at that point. It's only later you realise you have to work on a character and everything like I do now, at that point I was too busy just trying to get it right than do anything else and that's where the director is very important. But it's also the way Indian cinema is moving at the moment with the new generation of directors, new generation of thinkers and actors who are all willing to take certain risks and diverting into various different aspects within the parameters of Indian cinema and it's great."

Be it Dil Se, Kya Kehna or the technically brilliant and performance packed Mission Kashmir, Preity has always been associated with what are important and impact-making films. Her last path-breaking film was by newcomer Farhan Akhtar and resulted in not only a product that twisted a new angle to the way Indian films were being made, but also a subject that touched hearts and identified the now gener-asian.

"I'm very proud and happy to be associated with Dil Chahta Hai," enthuses Preity. "Because that was our voice you know, it was the new generation and the urban Indian youth and almost to an extent the yuppie Indian youth where we're just hanging out and doing stuff, trying to be independent. So when this guy who's a friend of mine, Farhan (Akhtar) decides to make a movie and we all get together with a 135 person crew it breaks a certain amount of usual norms, it broke away from the hero and heroine syndrome, we were only characters. That's really, really interesting because if it develops more then our cinema is going more international and much more faster. Because we're adapting and reaching out to various different audiences and not only the thinking that's confined to interiors and the villages in India which was initially what was happening. I think now, with the media opening up and the networks such as cable and satellite and the internet explosion, everything's changing, the viewership and thought process has changed and how they look at a film and perceive the product has changed, there's so much more awareness now."

Her films are international successes and her fan following in the overseas market is extraordinary, and with a grand show like India With Love which is aimed to cater to both an Asian and non-Asian audience, she finds herself once more contributing to something that is pushing Indian cinema further. Speaking in a voice that conceals a wry smile that says 'my lips are sealed', Preity tells me although she can't reveal what exactly this show will bring to the UK, she can definitely guarantee it'll be like nothing before.

"Well I don't think I can tell you what I've got planned for these shows, but I can assure you they're going to be very different in terms of creativity because it's not going to be your typical people coming on stage, lip-synching and miming to songs and leaving, there's much more creative input gone into it and we're working on scripts to give the essence of the Indian film industry in the films that we've done rather than just come, do a song and leave. Yes songs and music are a huge part of our culture and those are definitely going to be there but there are also going to be certain other things that will set the mood. Last year when Ash, Aamir and I did the world tour, everybody said it was different and they had seen a lot shows but never one with such creativity in it."

She accompanied Aamir and Aishwarya on the tour that rocked the US and was meant to come to our own shores, but September 11th changed the schedule and resulted in UK fans missing out, only to be compensated with what is set to be the biggest event of its kind ever to be held in the UK. I ask her to re-live the moment she first came out on stage in front of so many during her last tour and she energetically reveals:

"God I was so nervous! The first time I stepped out onto stage I had all this nervous energy popping out of my fingers, ears, feet, everywhere and my first two shows I

have no idea how I did them, but after that I sort of relaxed. It's all about having fun, that's the whole point!"
"There's a stage when you get overwhelmed by everything but there's a point when you just let it take over and get into and rise over the moment. That's when you feel your heart beat and the energy there is and it's the most amazing thing to be in front of a live audience, especially one that's reacting really well. The worst thing would be to be in front of an audience that's not reacting!"

From studying how criminal minds work to films to now performing in front of millions, Preity Zinta has come a long way. She's been central to path-breaking films and delivered performances that have earned her accolades and clearly shown she is here to stay. Her decision to take on different roles and make a difference is probably the biggest gamble a newcomer can take, but it's paid off and she has in a short span of time established herself as a constantly evolving and progressing actress.
"Thank you that means a lot, I don't come from a film background so my culture and way of thinking was different and I was studying criminal psychology. When I got into films everyone was teasing me 'Preity, please don't put on a white sari and start dancing' so it was a conscious effort from my side to do work that makes a difference, because you know cinema can make a difference. A normal person on the road can go and watch a movie and be completely moved by it. It can change his point of view or at least contribute to it, and that's the power of cinema. So it's a power that should be used positively and a medium that can have both substance and entertainment, that's why I always try to do roles that will make a difference, and sometimes I've succeeded and other times I've realised 'ok that wasn't right'."

"From playing to an unwed mother to my character in Dil Se which was a normal girl, probably one of the most normal girls on Indian film. The way she was so down to earth and so frank that she asked a guy 'are you a virgin' and says my boyfriend dumped me because he had to go to another place. From playing an unwed mother in Kya Kehna which I felt it was a good film that was not propaganda telling teenagers to go out and get pregnant, it was to say that we have to take responsibility for our actions and that our parents should support us in certain ways and increase awareness in certain ways. This was to say don't make the same mistake that this girl did and when something like this happens there's not just one person to be blamed. Then I played a cop in Sangharsh, which was different and quite crazy, Chori Chori Chupke Chupke where I played a prostitute - that was a bit full on though! So I'm trying to do different stuff, I don't know what works, it's really up to the audience, if the audience supports good films it makes it easier for us to encourage better film. If they go and support a really silly filmi cheesy film I'm going to kill half of them! Because then there's twenty more of these silly cheesy films coming out and instead of moving forward you're taking a few steps back! So it's important for the audience to support us and good, intelligent cinema, like the West where great films do well and so they think of making five more great films."

"So now if a love story does well they want to make five more love stories and if a cheesy film works they want to make ten more of them because they believe in the formula system that if one film works it'll work again."

Defying predictions and conventions the young actress has much more in store and hasn't even finished her first innings yet. With her it's one long take that endures and entertains. As she reveals what's in store, she can't hide her infectious enthusiasm of every film she mentions.

"One film is Rakesh Roshan's Koi Mil Gaya with Hrithik, which will be the world's first special effects sci-fi film that is a musical. I think that'll be something very, very different. It's incredible how it'll be, it's going to be a fantasy, it'll break your heart, it's going to make you smile and cheer the human spirit, it has everything. Then there's a film called The Hero with Sunny Deol, directed by Anil Sharma, it's a film about espionage and is a spy thriller. Then I'm doing a film with Honey Irani called Armaan which we haven't started yet but will have Anil Kapoor and Gracey. I have a film also ready to release now which is called Dil Hai Tumhara, the promos are going to start now in the next few weeks."

"I'm looking forward to that film because it's the first time a character like the one I play is appearing no the big screen. Usually when you have a heroine she plays a character limited to a heroine, but this time I'm playing someone who's a complete tomboy. And it's not a tomboy who dresses in saris and has long hair, it's a real tomboy. I cut my hair for the movie and have short hair to my ears now, in it I play a complete rebel, a compulsive liar, attention seeker and a total liar. It's a very deprived and interesting character, the kind that has the undertones of never getting love and always wanting that love. A girl who wants to do everything right but has all the wrong ways of doing it. I'm really looking forward to it because it's a comedy and a tragedy and it'll make you both laugh and cry and feel for the character."

Before wrapping up and wishing her well, I ask how she's enjoying the film circus that is Cannes. This year sees India making its mark as not only are Raj Kapoor's films being felicitated and Devdas being premiered, but also Asoka and K3G are being screened and the international, particularly Hollywood press are lapping up the Indian magic. Preity of course, is having a blast too.

"Well yesterday was this India Day party which was quite nice, and Devdas is really happening. I was actually going to come back early but then thought since I'm here I may as well stay and see Devdas."

"I'm so happy that Indian cinema is coming of age and going global, and that an awareness is increasing. There are so many people you meet here; I don't even remember their names! It's like a sea of faces and so many cards being given into your hand, which all go into my bag, then I get back and look at them and say 'who was that??'! But it's great, it's absolutely crazy! It's incredible how they do marketing in the West and how these people work. It's good to be here and it's an experience."

As I end my conversation with the pretty young actress, I ask her to leave readers with some words she'd like to convey and she pauses for a second before using this interview to deliver a positive message to all too.

"Look forward to something really different and that you have never seen before in Hyde Park or Manchester! If there's anything I'd really like to say to the readers it's that people blend better than governments, so it's time we put aside these petty affairs and got together as one world, lived our lives, had fun and enjoyed ourselves, and of course, enjoy the show!"

Fuad Omar

GOLDEN BOY: HRITHIK ROSHAN

Hrithik Roshan is only three years old. The man who every Asian recognises, has
at one time or the other mimicked and has been a part of his craze at some point since Jan 2000 is still one of the most media savvy people around. The press hound him and write as much about him as they can, and even sell magazines by just plastering his face on the cover, and in a short span of time he arrived on the scene, caused hysteria and became a target of the expected 'Does he live up to the hype' articles. So what makes Hrithik tick and is he really Bollywood's golden boy?

When Kaho Na Pyaar Hai released no one could ignore the hunky demi-god whose posters were everywhere in a tight tee shirt and dark glasses, flexing his bicep-bulging arm around another newcomer, Amisha Patel. There was much industry scepticism, could a newcomer really make it in an age of established heroes, and if not what would happen when the current crop of actors decided to take it easy for a while? A lot of hopes were pinned on the pair since their launch vehicle was from a respected hit-filmmaker and they looked fresh. Rakesh Roshan even stated at the time, "I hope the audience accepts them because the industry needs new blood," which he said not only as a father, but as a filmmaker. The pre-release campaign began with lilting tunes highlighted in the promos, set to a backdrop of scenes showcasing what was to be a visual treat: Rakesh Roshan had gone out of his way to make sure he had a polished product that was aesthetically pleasing and the care in lighting, camera angles and even colour co-ordination is there for all to see.

The film drew hoards and what was dubbed as 'overnight success' meant the film and its stars were a craze not only in their hometown, but across the world. As Hrithik himself told me, all it took was the moment the audience accepted him to change his life, and that was one moment he would never forget:

"I entered the theatre with everybody and some people recognised me and said 'hey you're the actor in the film!' and I was like 'yeah' and they were like 'all the best' and I just said 'thank you'. I entered with them and sat with them. And when the film got over there was a stampede, I was mobbed. They had to call the police force, there was a crowd of thousands outside the theatre and the next show got cancelled and delayed. They could not get me out of the theatre and they had to call guards and pull me out because there were people everywhere."
Every time he tells this story his eyes glaze with that soft light that shines in the film and he recounts it as though he was a third person at the scene, in disbelief at what was happening.

"And I couldn't get out of the place, they had to call people there and put me in a different car and just whisk me away. I was with my friends and I kept asking them 'What's this? What's happening? Is this normal? Does this happen with everybody? What's this?' and we were all stunned and they didn't know what to tell me, they just said 'Yeah this is good, just enjoy yourself!' and I didn't know what to make of it. It was like instant fame. Three hours. That's all it took to change my life. Just three hours."

He still can't believe it and still thanks God for that moment which is one few are blessed with.
Hrithik and Amisha became stars and immediately the suitcases of neatly-packed training they had endured and given everything to over the past few years were ceremoniously ignored by anyone who wrote about them. "OVERNIGHT SENSATION!" screamed newspapers as though this man had just walked into a film, been shot well and was handed a label that said star. Hrithik was not amused.

Getting used to the media invasion that follows stars is never easy. If you're shy, you can't be anymore. You'll sometimes have to meet a stranger and let them ask you questions you're totally unprepared for and if you fumble or can't deliver a near-perfect quote in the first instance it will be held against you. Try it. Another extremely popular Indian film journalist and myself often play the game where we interview each other and endure being on the receiving end of a good grilling and it's never easy coming up with quotable answers. There's a saying that the sweet isn't as sweet without tasting the sour and Hrithik was made to go through what would probably be the most difficult period of his life. His film was a phenomenal hit which was great, overnight he became the biggest thing his country had seen but that also meant he no longer had a private life nor could he go out anywhere without being mobbed: his freedom was exchanged for fame.

Things took an ugly turn when his father was shot and that too because his hard work paid off and his film was a success, by people who have still to this day not been caught. Hrithik kept a bedside vigil and even contemplated giving up acting altogether because the price and stakes are too high when family is involved, but he found the strength to get through and not let the bad guys win. His personal tragedy stole the limelight from him, not allowing him to fully process the success of his film and what this meant, and soon he found himself cringing when every magazine cover would put him on the cover for no rhyme or reason and TV shows where he appeared asked the viewer 'Can you handle it?' if they showed you Hrithik Roshan every ad break. What followed KNPH was not only a media circus but an explosion and only casualty-toll was personal. Hype surrounded whatever the megastar would do and he was called everything from the next Amitabh Bachchan to being reported as giving Shah Rukh sleepless nights, but he took everything in his stride. He told me on the sets of Kabhi Khushi Kabhie Gham:

"I knew it was just not the truth. Luckily for me I had the intelligence to know that what was going on was irresponsible and dishonest, because they (the press) were putting me up to levels of experienced persons in the business when I had just started with my first film, and even in that I wasn't that good."

His next release was Khalid Mohammed's Fiza which meant the actor would be shot by none other than the technically brilliant Santosh Sivan and share screen time with greats such as Karisma Kapoor and Jaya Bachchan. Despite a widespread and very clear division of the audience the film proved what Hrithik's detractors feared: he was not a one hit wonder and could not only act, but act very well. His sensitive yet volatile performance as Aman, the son who can no longer distinguish between right and wrong and seeks his own brand of justice won him accolades over, despite many taking out personal vendettas against Khalid's film due to his years of film criticism. The film saw Hrithik delivering a mature performance that no one expected, and to an extent this worked against him with the younger audience. The children who went to see Fiza didn't understand or want to see their favourite actor angry or crying, they only wanted to see him laugh, dance and be the 'hero'. The film achieved mediocre success but echoed its points through and through, reaffirming its stars mastery of their art in the process. Mission Kashmir was released among a lot of hype that brought it into a clash with Aditya Chopra's Mohabbatein and many sections of the press saw this as the chance to live out their Shah Rukh vs Hrithik fantasies as the two films released on the same day. Mission Kashmir is powerful, got a good response and is Vinod Chopra's most financially rewarding film to date, yet any talk of the film would be in the same breath as a comparison with the success of Mohabbatein and so once more Hrithik's growth as an actor was suppressed as the box office returns of the two films dominated the dailies. Many say Hrithik should have stuck to hero roles for a while, but to pass up the opportunity to work with filmmakers with a vision and that too in a role that is challenging is a sacrifice of a chance that doesn't come round twice.

In 2001 Hrithik had just two releases, one was the forgettable Subhash Ghai film Yaadein which for whatever reasons had bad editing, a wafer thin screenplay and banked more on its stars than its content, and Kabhi Khushi Kabhie Gham. Yaadein's failure at the box office was not a setback for Hrithik although many took it as the end of his career, because as an artiste he performed as he was asked to and even stole certain scenes. K3G is the next phenomenon in Hrithik's life and whereas many have tried to criticise his decision to be in such a huge canvas and take on such a role, the film and his contribution to it worked. Without taking from Karan Johar's magnum opus, but focussing on the actor I'm writing about, Hrithik's You Are My Soniya is to this day one of the most downloaded dance songs since its release. The choreography gave the audience another chance to see the magic he can work when in Farah Khan's capable hands and his performance was underrated as he moved the audience to tears when he entered his brother's house in London for the first time and also gave his all to his character without taking too much from the film so the balance was shifted. What he was asked to do he did with great success and achieving another milestone in his career. He held screen time with stalwarts of Indian cinema and contributed to some of the most moving scenes seen on celluloid and is proud of the result.

Hrithik's last few films were the forgettable Aap Mujhe Achchey Lagne Lage, Na Tum Jaano Na Hum which again did not set the box office on fire and Kunal Kohli's Mujhse Dosti Karoge which suffered at the hands of many factors, none being the actors. Every actor during his career goes through a lean phase, but for Hrithik these films are just the teething pangs that he missed out on when he began his career, and there is no lean phase to speak of. When he goes out, he's still the most photographed and adored star, and overseas in the UK all his films have done enough business to enter the UK box office top 20 in their opening weekends, including Aap Mujhe Achchey Lagne Lage, meaning he still holds that pull and loyal fan base some magazines would have you believe he's lost. Anyone who witnessed his first world tour will testify to his electrifying live performances as arguably being the best by any actor of our generation. He set the stage on fire time and again, venue after venue and night after night in what became a gruelling schedule, all without a whimper of a complaint. After being re-introduced to him backstage he gave me a huge hug and told me he was a fan of mine and he had been reading my work. That single moment I was speechless and I felt humbled like never before. Here was the world's biggest superstar at this point in time, about to go on stage and create hysteria for the umpteenth time and backstage he was confessing to be a fan of my work. I can't even find words to describe what that feels like.

Hrithik's professionalism, dedication to living up to his fans expectations and genuineness are all not only signs of his humility, but exactly who he has been even before he entered the film industry. I first met him in 2001 and two years later every time I meet him he is as warm, as affectionate and looking better by the day.

His work in Sooraj Barjatya's film Main Premi ki Deewani Hoon is apparently mindblowing and Koi Mil Gaya is one of the year's most anticipated films with an air of curiosity surrounding it rather than the ridicule the media predicted when they prematurely revealed what the film's subject was. Hrithik has no inkling of tiring soon. A book 'inspired' by him entitled Bollywood Boy released last year and he is already being touted as a legend, so is Hrithik on his way out? No way. When I first met him I told him I may one day write a book on him but I felt it was too early at this stage because his growth would be steady and one that would see many more milestones. I've constantly smiled at allegations of him being a legend already because I know his journey has only just completed its first phase and there's so much more in store for him. So what makes Hrithik tick? His drive, his dedication, his family and his wife.

Meeting Suzanne is definitely one of the memorable experiences I've had. The minute she talks to you her sweetness shines through. When she arrived on the sets of K3G as the scene when Hrithik is telling Jugal he is leaving to meet his two girlfriends, she loved being there. Watch Hrithik and you know he still can't take his eyes off her. Even while watching the rushes of some scenes or getting his outfit ready his eye is always on Suzanne to make sure she's ok and it's honestly one of the sweetest things to see. He is completely in love with her and she with him and it shows. Hrithik Roshan is not only a sensation of Indian cinema that has just completed one phase of his career but he is also someone many have yet to get under the skin of. There's so much more to the man than what's written about him. His love for his father shone through when he spoke of him in awe and catch him in between shots singing songs or posing for photos with fans and that's what's not written about. Is Hrithik Roshan Bollywood's golden boy? I don't know, but I know one thing: he's here for a very long time.

Fuad Omar

Film Review: Kal Ho Naa Ho

Kal Ho Naa Ho is a hip fusion of a heartwarming story and masterful direction executed to the nth degree with razor sharp precision by ace new director Nikhil Advani that sets a new standard of cinema, (NOT Indian cinema, but CINEMA), achieving instant pop-culture status within minutes of the film beginning.

Pop culture references, a very tightly woven array of sequences adapted from a brilliant screenplay by Karan Johar that has got to be his best yet, coupled with riveting and oft-touching dialogues courtesy of Niranjan Iyengar, KHNH is the perfect cinematic offering for any film buff craving a feast of a good movie.

Newcomer Nikhil Advani graduates from assisting on previous Bolly blockbusters such as Mohabbatein, Kuch Kuch Hota Hai and K3G, and in a path-breaking debut etches his name on every frame of the film, lacing it with caricature plot devices, breathtaking devices that drive the film forward and a peppy soundtrack that has everybody tapping their feet by the end of the film, that is, if you still have any control over your emotions. Advani creates an ambience that sets its own standards and revolutionises cinema. The character interviews with the camera that are cut to frequently throughout the film are a nice touch that works, and successfully pulls the viewer further into Nikhil's world, which has a setting, a mood, colourful characters and through these 'camera conversations' an intimate encounter between audience and character that enhances the interactive symbiotic relationship in the medium of film and fan.

The Kantiben thread is hilarious, with musical accompaniements and chants oozing like icing on a well-creamed cake. The Spielbergesque homage of the classic 'shot of doom' scene where Catherine realises Aman's predicament and the camera zooms in on her while pulling away akin to the world distancing itself from Roy Schneider in Jaws is again evidence we are clearly dealing with a man who knows his field, medium and craft.

Nikhil has taken every major popular cultural facet and that too at its origin of America and made it his own, creating a film destined to be referenced as a pop cultural phenomenon in itself. From 70s disco to the 80s revolution, through to holding the emotional thread that neatly dangles your emotions before your eyes for a good ten minutes in the climax before cutting the strings in a sharp snip that leaves not a single dry eye in the audience, Kal Ho Naa Ho is nothing short of a brilliant debut from a talented and meticulous filmmaker. Advani has brought emotions out that have enjoyed lesser successful translations on screen previously, and extracts from his performers performances that break new ground and draw a line unparalleled by anything they've done before, Shah Rukh included. We may have seen him cry a hundred times before, but never like this, never with the desperation of a dying man as Nikhil has gotten out of him and never mouthed such ethereal romantic eternal lines as he so non-chalantly does which shows the quiet director who has the loudest voice on the sets has much to offer the future of film.

KHNH is not just a film, it is a cult film, and as with all cult phenomena they only continue to inspire for generations after their time. Watch for Nikhil Advani because kal ho naa ho, he very rightly rules today, and will do for many years to come...

Fuad Omar

RAISING UNIVERSAL AWARENESS

Hounslow's Montague Hall hosted a cancer awareness conference last Thursday, graced with the presence of ex-Miss Universe Sushmita Sen, where people from Harrow, Wembley, Wealdstone and all over London gathered in aid of a good cause.

The young Indian beauty was invited by 22 year old student Haresh Sood to help raise funds for the Imperial Cancer Research Fund and other cancer charities, by participating in a public conference designed to raise awareness to the plight of millions.

"This is not a glamorous event where I come and sing or dance on stage or any of those things, but where we wanted to bring forward the seriousness of the matter," she told the audience of nearly 200. "Seeing you all here is honestly, for me, a grand success, because all of you sitting here today have made a difference to someone's life."

The conference was based around the theme of cancer awareness and a live broadcast on Asianet the night before had brought with it a tremendous response. One terminally ill gentleman who saw the television interview was so touched to see this model-turned-actress appealing to all to support this charity, that he phoned in immediately pledging a donation and thanked the efforts Haresh Sood and his team were investing in this worthwhile fund. His presence at the conference was one that moved Sushmita to tears as he told her, "Being a cancer patient, and seeing you show such support, it touched me so much. You have given me so much confidence through your appeal and support that I am sure I will write to you soon telling you my cancer is gone", said Mr Agha, causing many to shed a tear and give him a thunderous applause.

The audience expressed their appreciation for the actress' honesty about her own ignorance of cancer, her openness with them on her career and her attempt to raise money for research into this life-threatening disease, as she expressed how she was not the larger-than-life character they had seen on screen, but a girl placed in different circumstances.

"Basically I'm a very average girl, I have been very lucky in my life. There is not much difference between you and me, my feelings your feelings, my fears and your fears, your loves and hates and my loves and hates, except that they (the press) write a lot about me, good and bad things, and it's just a spotlight above my head, otherwise I'm very much like you."

Money raised was donated to Imperial Cancer Research Fund and Wish upon A Star Foundation for terminally ill children who have a wish they would like fulfilled in their lifetime. Sushmita made one such child's dream of meeting a Bollywood star come true when she met her at her bedside in hospital.

Haresh Sood, a veteran fund raiser who has created his own company for charity work, which celebrates it's 5th anniversary with this event, was extremely pleased with the evening's success.

"I am very happy with the way the event has gone and has raised awareness as we wanted. People have enjoyed tonight and most of all, it's all for a good cause. From here we go to Bradford, Leicester and Birmingham for more conferences and then this whole tour climaxes in Nottingham with a musical show where Sushmita is a guest," he said enthusiastically.

Well-wishers, fans and concerned supporters waved goodbye to their shining star as she left wishing everyone a good night, and no one left disappointed with their meeting. For one night only, London had been graced by a beautiful starlet from a universe far, who welcomed a personal interaction with those who ventured out to catch a glimpse of her. There were no lights, no fancy show or musical interlude, for tonight Sushmita Sen had descended not to dazzle and to entertain a crowd, but to shed light on a cause which needs support and cannot be ignored.

Fuad Omar

From right to left: Fuad Omar, Sushmita Sen, bodyguard Sandeep, Haresh Sood, Raina Sood and their fundraising team

SUSHMITA SEN: AN INNER VIEW

Sushmita Sen is someone who has always had her feet firmly planted on the ground and be it her accessibility to fans, her keenness to talk about her films or whatever opportunity she gets to speak out for worthy causes, she does so whenever possible. Her rise in Bollywood is also meteoric. From Dastak to Biwi No.1 to Filhaal may have been a journey of few films, but was a well travelled long road which she used to improve on each performance and attain a position to be reckoned with. She is now an eternal superstar who's name alone adds prestige to any project she's associated with. She's an ex-Miss India, ex-Miss Universe, supermodel and currently one of Bollywood's hottest stars. This particular meeting with this soaring star which has always been archived for a special publication (and sees light of day exclusively in Asian Xpress) was one which left its mark, as I got to experience a touch of the magical glitter she has sprinkled on so many. I recall it from the banks of my memory that won't let me be and wrestles to be released. All those who have constantly asked for more on Sushmita, you got your wish.

The actress seen on screen, the supermodel men dream of and the shooting star who rises with her every success are all guises of the model-turned-actress often portrayed in the media. Today I had met the real Sushmita Sen, the person and not the myth, and was fortunate enough to find her to be beyond what she is made out to be, and truly someone worthy of the Miss Universe title, not on the strength of her beauty alone. Excerpts from our conversation:

"What's it like to be Fuad?" she playfully asks as she catches a glimpse of my first question, turning me into the interviewee. Good, I tell her considering I am in the company of an angel others dream of meeting. Her dazzling smile and piercing eyes flash at me, as she browses through photographs from our last meeting at one of her film's premieres.

"Why am I not in this photo?" she asks pointing to my coverage of one of her previous blockbuster premieres. "But it's a good photo, you're very photogenic," she tells me drawing attention away from my questions and making me lose almost any track of thought.

Before we sidetrack any further I choose to dive straight into the interview and ignore my starting question which she has already used, and begin with the questions.

Sushmita Sen has come a long way since her career began. From ex-Miss Universe to supermodel to top actress, now she has achieved a position from where she can make a difference and bring joy to many because of her high profile celebrity status.
"If through being a well-recognised personality you can bring someone happiness, it's a very good feeling. Just by meeting someone or highlighting an issue I can make an impression, and it is God's blessings."

Throughout the interview one thing has come through: Sushmita Sen is a very humble and spiritual person. She constantly utters the words "Inshallah" (God-willing) and

"God's blessings", making it impossible to have a conversation with her without remembering God, who she feels eternally grateful to and is very mindful of.

"My cousin Peeku and I, used to go outside Hajji Ali's place, in Bombay, and sit on the pavement and I used to wish 'Just once please get me up there into the pageant, I don't mind if I don't win, but just get me there in the top 10 so the world can see me' and it was God's Grace that in May 1994 I represented India in the Miss Universe pageant," she recalls smiling. "And I don't know how but I won it! Out of 88 girls who were all marvellous, I won it!" she says enthralled, and full of laughter.

"I am from a lower middle class, and conservative family where I wasn't allowed after 8pm, if I was staying at a friends house I'd have to leave the number, etc. I started to realise whatever they do they do because they love you so much. At the age of 15 I saw people on television and decided I wanted to be famous. I used to watch Miss India and tell my daddy, 'If I was in her place I'd answer like this' and he used to be like 'Haan, aisi to baitkur sab ko baathey karna aata hain, kuch karkey dikao' and I took that as a challenge."

"At the age of 17 I was at this function and this gentleman came up to me and said 'Aapko Miss India join karna chaye', and I was like, 'haan, haan, zaroor'! Then he said he was serious, so I went the next morning to the Times of India office and filled in the form. I cried so much that night because I thought that was the biggest disaster of my life and that so many people would see me because it is televised, key log mujhe pasand karenge to kya hoga, log nahin pasand krenge to kya hoga, and then I reached the

Miss India finals in 1994. And it was after winning this title I went for Ms Universe," she recalls with a glow in her eyes.

"I hope to utilise the platform God has given me for causes that can do with my help, I have worked for many charities in the past and I don't want to say I am working specifically for one or the other. It is true for that UK visit you mentioned earlier I was there for cancer research, but for me to even make a statement would be wrong, because like many people I was ignorant about cancer, but came to help create awareness and get people to support the Imperial Cancer Research Fund and such charities for the work that they do."

And that she did, the charity side of her is not one widely reported in the press, but the dazzling beauty does so much for so many and that too thanks to the charming person that she is and she's aware that being a celebrity helps.

"It feels great to be able to bring someone joy. If through being a recognised well-known or little-known personality, if through being who you are you can make a difference to someone, it's a very good feeling. I never really thought it was possible for one person to make a lot of people happy, and when I read about it in magazines and such I didn't believe it. But when it happens to you, you really realise the implications and the importance of it, and it's all God's blessings that you are able to bring some happiness to someone," she says tactfully avoiding speaking too much of the good deeds she does, believing actions speak louder than words.

Her face shows how humbled she is by the importance given to her through her status, and she reinforces her belief how she can give back what love she has earned, by contributing to others happiness. She pauses before responding to my question on how this status has changed her life, and offers an honest confession.

"I know when I look in the mirror today I'm a different person than who I was five or seven years ago, I'm hoping it's for the better! There's a whole lot of differences in terms of my perspective towards life, my very basic existence as a person, my level of confidence, my level of dependence, everything has changed with time. I'm more independent; I'm financially more independent, whereas before my father used to buy me gifts, now I can afford to buy my father gifts! So I know I'm a different person," she says smiling, as she reflects on the past few years that have given her success, fame and recognition.

I point out how Sushmita Sen, the person and not the star, is emerging, and this brief encounter is turning into a rare insight of not the characters she plays on screen, or her image but who she is. Again she dishes me her brilliant smile and explains this idea of an 'image', which creeps into audience's minds.

"Cinema is larger than life, in that everybody is ten times bigger, in not just terms of their physical appearance, but also their basic personality is so much bigger, on a 70mm. When the fans see you on-screen, they're imagining you're the 'wife' or 'sister' or 'daughter' or whatever character it is, you can imagine it in your mind. But when the same person comes in front of you as Sushmita, as Fuad, as whoever, suddenly that myth is broken and what you're seeing is a person, and you don't know what to expect from that person, so it can be a scary feeling. Some people when they become stars develop attitude and want to distance people from themselves, but our basic business of being in this business is to be close to people, and if being in cinema is going to push us away from people then that's the wrong profession," she analyses wisely.

Filhaal gained Sushmita Sen rave reviews, but failed to ignite the box office back home possibly due to a daringly different subject or something else, but internationally it hit the bullseye. The media business is such that you're constantly having to justify yourself, does she feel her days of proving a point are over?
"In every creative person's life you are always proving a point. In this business you are constantly proving a point, you could have 10 hit films and all eyes are on the 11th film to see if it does well, and if it doesn't they (the media) will say 'Arrey, yeh nahin chali!' so you are always proving a point," she reasons.

Every interview has its moments, its magic, but at the end of it, it all boils down to numbers: 'cut it down, edit it from here, we'll put a picture there'. So before this magical meeting is ended abruptly, I'll promise to give you more from the enchanting Sushmita soon, and leave you with 'The Sushmita I Know' penned by Sushmita Sen.

"She is an Indian from Bengal,
She is from a country that teaches love and respect for all,
She is a girl of 18, yet a child at heart,
Even now she loves to play those games which used to be a part of her childhood art
She loves little children and she envies them bad,
Because to this one stage she can never go back.

She is a dreamer of a kind with a wish to make them come
true,
She is a writer of a kind who wishes to create something
new,
She doesn't believe in ambition but what she aspires to be,
She aspires to be successful in whichever line she might
be,
She is jolly, sometimes upset, coping up with the ups and
downs,
And whatever life has to offer one must wear as a crown,
Her motto in life are the lines of Shakespeare,
"Life is not a midsummer night's dream,
Nor is it a tempest, it is but a comedy of errors,
So you live it as you like it,
Hence love one, love all, now and forever."
This is Sushmita as I know her.

- Sushmita Sen"

WITNESSING THE SUBI SAMUEL - SUSHMITA SEN MAGIC

It's a sunny Tuesday afternoon and the quiet studio in Versova seems unassuming and ordinary. Inside, history is about to be made as one of the most beautiful personalities to grace the silver screen is about to weave a web of glamour, class and unbound passion.

At 2pm sharp, Sushmita Sen arrives at the studio of Subi Samuel. Wearing a body hugging black dress and a smile that lit up all around her, she settles into the room which would witness her many metamorphisms in the next few hours. Looking a little nervous Subi talks her through a few concepts and suggests a few new looks before she lets him know what she has in mind. At 2:15 the designer and couturier extraordinaire Reza Shariffi arrives sporting a white tee and blue denims, dragging with him a bag full of the day's costumes. The clock hits 2:30 and the oversized fans are set up for a blowing effect on Sushmita's hair, which is almost ready. The studio is already undergoing the transformation into the abode where the forthcoming photo shoot will take place and the air is thick with tension. I ask Shraddha, Reza's assistant, how she feels.

"It's as though we're at a board exam or something," she says, "it's so quiet and everyone's working so hard."

She's absolutely right as the atmosphere is writhing with a sense of anticipation similar to the feeling that something big is about to happen.

Sushmita's hair is done and work starts on her make-up and look, while Subi walks in and out of the studio, checking all the equipment is set up as planned. Stealing a smile while looking a little anxious he turns to me and says:

"I hope you're ready for this. It's going to be quite an experience."
Nothing could have prepared me for the afternoon's shoot with Sushmita Sen.

It's 4:45 and Sushmita's make up is done. The simple ethereal princess has been transformed into a glamorous glowing queen before our eyes and is looking nothing short of stunning. The studio is set and she is raring to go and so begins the gruelling session which will immortalise the young beauty in a few pictures as she creates magic to everyone's delight in a manner no one is prepared for.

She walks in to the studio and takes centre stage before the camera. As the music starts and the camera begins to click, she rises phoenix-like wearing a gold creation sensually draping her heavenly body. The dress which is her own, envelopes her in its mouth showing her off to the hilt, as the music plays on full volume. She transforms before everyone's eyes into a beacon of life with her body responding to every beat and her eyes dancing like fireflies to the rhythm resonating within the camera's cavern. She literally stuns everyone into silence displaying clearly how expertly she controls her look and is still not only one of the world's topmost models but with the emotion screaming within her eyes for escape, how she is an amazing actress also. Subi clicks furiously calling out to her to let her know how wonderful she is looking. The studio's lights illuminate her as the moon does the earth and in turn everyone else present basks in her glow and beauty, as the world stops and nothing is as important as the moment that is now, the moment Sushmita Sen is weaving her own magic before the camera, and Subi is framing every sensational shot.

Fans blow her hair back as with her mouth slightly open she looks deep within the camera, it is clear that without the fans cooling things down, the studio would be steaming with the passion she is giving off. Her hair open and a fire in her eyes, Sushmita Sen is a lethal cocktail of elegance, beauty and class, seducing the camera with her every breath, ensuring every time the shutter clicks a masterpiece is captured. Subi okays the first session giving the go-ahead to change, as he winds his camera and shouts orders to his assistants preparing for the next shot and the rest of us watch in awe at the supermodel who casually strolls out, ready for her costume change. Subi is a master of his domain. His command over still moments when life is in motion is breathtaking, as he knows exactly how he wants every backdrop, every light and every prop.

I turn to my pad to jot a few notes of what just happened, barely recovering from the tornado which just scooped us up into her world and left us gasping for more while drowning in her scorching eyes. In no time it's 5:15pm and Sushmita walks in to the studio again, this time causing everyone's jaws to drop to the ground at what she's wearing. Chainmail armour adorns her with an ancient helmet crowning her head, allowing only a few tresses of her straight black hair to be seen. She carries a sword and is transformed completely from what she was minutes ago as we witness the birth of a Samurai warrior complete with a look which would send any army into retreat. Wearing a black dhoti and giving the camera a piercing look, making it impossible to distinguish which is sharper – her eyes or the sword – she strikes what can only be described as deadly authentic poses. Her feet reflect a bold stance as each foot acts as a pivot for her body weight and she gives a daring battle-like look, as though she could have just run straight out of a Hollywood epic. The fans are off as everyone just stares at the costume which fits her to a tee, and wonder how Reza came up with such a masterpiece creation. She jumps into a series of majestic poses holding the sword above her head, between her eyes and handling it as if it was an extension of her body. I stare deep into the eyes which penetrate the camera lens and find myself lost in thoughts wondering whether she is about to be knighted or should I kneel before her seeking a knighthood.

The suit shows her like a true crusader, reflecting some of her personality as warriors wandering spirits dance around her as she cuts through them with ease. Her trusty blade of steel slices through the air with great dignity and her eyes show she is clearly ready for battle as well as victory. The spirits of King Arthur, Knights of the Round Table and Joan of Arc all prostrate before her, jousting in mid air before her eyes as she draws on inspiration which must be from deep within, appearing like a mystery possessed.

"Awesome!" shouts Subi, as she gets on the ground stretching in every flexible direction and enacts a taandav of her own, exorcising any demons which may haunt her.

194

The armour hangs off her body as though it was made for her and in between every seven shots it is slightly readjusted by her team who ensure in every frame she is ready for battle. The room again turns into an awe-struck audience as our eyes drink from the golden gauntlet that is Sushmita, intoxicating us to a whole new level. Commanding attention with her every gaze, she poses in what can only be described as incarnations reflecting the epitome of a surviving warrior doing battle to avoid knightfall. Her helmet comes off as she looks at everyone's stunned faces and announces, "now we're really going to have some fun!" with a wicked smile, making you wonder if this Heavenly Angel could be the devil in disguise.

She goes on to play with the sword, juggling it meticulously between poses which seem to be effortlessly executed and in perfect precision. She dazzles us with her swordplay which is being captured by the camera while flashing galaxies swirl within her eyes as the magic she weaves comes alive across the room.

In between shots I approach her, sensing the wizardry, and marvel at how she manages to do so much in a restricting costume.

'Is it heavy,' I ask, to which she shrugs and laughs, saying with a hint of sarcasm "Heavy? No!" trying to catch her breath, before flashing the sensational Sen smile my way and surprising us with her endless energy as she gets up announcing, "These will be the wacky ones now…!"

And with that she launches into 20 different poses crouching and balancing while staying close to the ground, all while handling her armour, dhoti and accessories in a way which demands applause. Before the final shot of this second change is canned, she looks straight through the camera lens into Subi's soul, her eyes brimming with electricity, giving a look stating clearly that no matter how many battles she loses, the war she will win. Subi lets out an ecstatic scream, climaxing at the perfect shot and regains his breath as the next change begins.

6:30pm sees the beginning of the third costume's shoot and Subi is desperately fixing up the lighting for a series of close-ups. The side of his eyes are alive with passion as he smiles reassuringly when I ask if all shoots are like this one, which has stunned everyone present (and that consists of people who work on shoots everyday) to which he replies, "Only Sushmita's!" before asking his assistant to change the background to a green colour.

The tired faces show how much this particular photo shoot is sizzling with energy and draining everyone, except Sushmita who is all set for the next shot, walking into the studio in a black slinky dress. A few close-ups are taken before Reza adds a green choker to her neck excited at the Polaroid approval Subi promptly provides. The blower fans are again on and Sushmita looks up into the lens with a sensuality that would put Madonna to shame, using her eyes to dance around every click and lips to pout at every given opportunity. Mesmerising with her every gaze, she focuses deep on the camera and photographer as Subi marvels at his muse's tenacity, beaming that his every shot is surpassing expectations. Gold drapes are added to the shot by Reza who ensures she is still looking fresh although her smile shows no sign of fading. Subi asks her to convey innocence and she looks up with eyes of a child, coming straight from the soul of the little girl who has been forced to grow up in a world she has conquered many times over. When asking for emotion it takes her just seconds to look into the camera misty-eyed, tears forming in each window to her soul and give a look which proves not only her amazing acting capabilities but also her ability to stir emotion in the hardest of hearts.

The shot okayed she leaves to change for the next set of close-ups, leaving everyone tired and pondering where she gets the energy from, given her and Subi are performing the most difficult tasks. Emerging in a pink sequinned tube top, the close-ups are taken against a pink lit background which adds a unique effect to the pictures, and again he asks her to execute a rainbow of emotions. He suggests and experiments with a few shots involving cling-film wrapped around her shoulders before gasping with exhaustion and announcing "OK, fantastic! Pack-up!" in a manner akin to a sonic boom ending the madness.

Sushmita walks back to change and the rest of us remain firmly rooted to the ground, in awe of the two geniuses who had scooped us up into their world for a day. I had asked Subi prior to the sessions what his shoots were like and his reply was:

"They are all hard work, involving a lot of effort. But in all honesty, no shoot is like Sushmita's. She gives her all and it's like a whole new experience. After shooting with her you feel so satisfied and drained, nothing can prepare you for it."

He was right. Everyone was exhausted and witnessing a Sushmita Sen shoot is like going into the mouth of a volcano before you know it's about to erupt. It was now clear to see how this Miss Universe turned model turned actress had conquered every venture that had come her way: with pure, unbridled, sizzling passion.

The cosmic energy she exuded is beyond words and the ease with which she conveyed the most soul-stirring of emotions and look so good only proved her limitless reservoir of acting talent and that it is true what they say:
No one shoots like Sushmita Sen. It is an experience like no other.

Fuad Omar

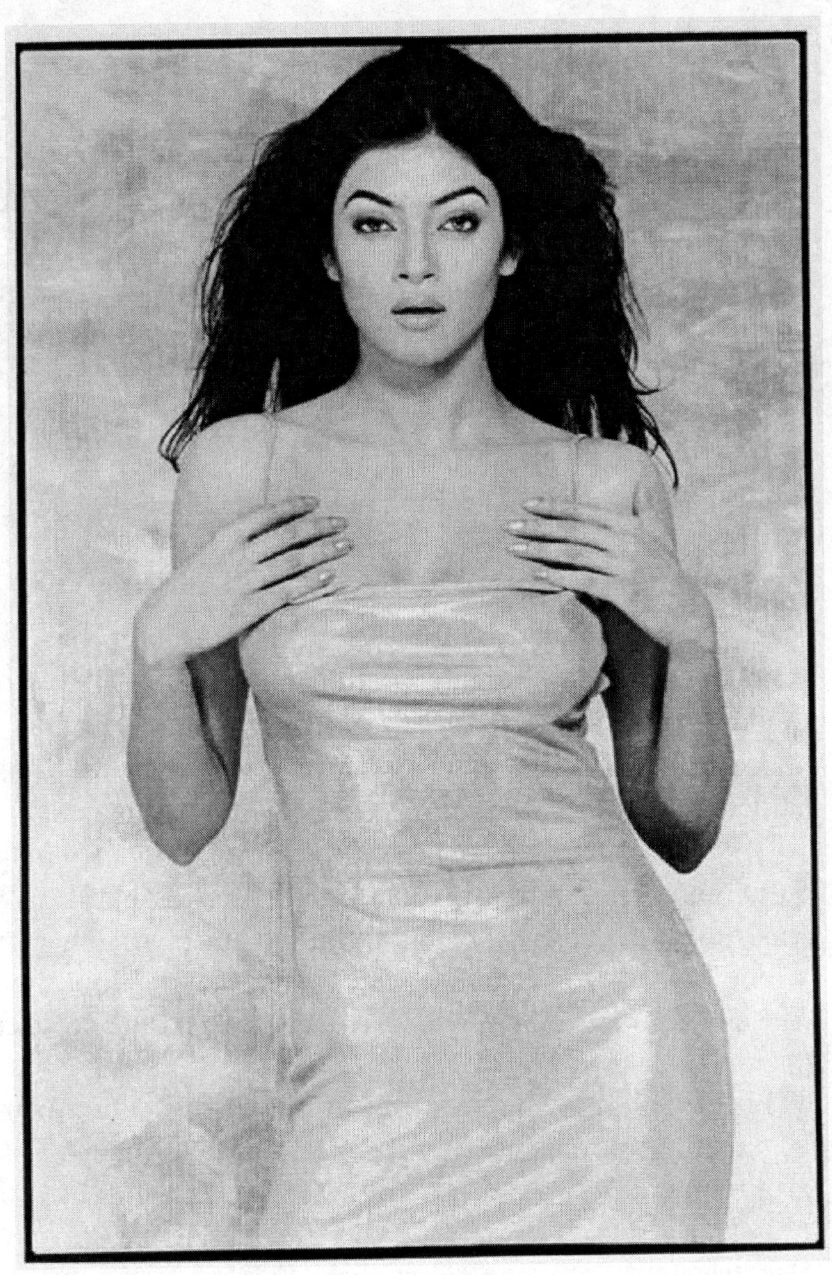

Into the Den: A Photoshoot with Subi Samuel

A bright spark burns like an inferno engulfing everything in its path, allowing the quiet but empowering genesis of a life. The spark is in Subi Samuel's eye and the creation his idea. Like a curse it breeds in his mind causing restlessness until it sees form in a manner close to its conception culminating in a photograph which matches the image in his minds' eye close to perfection.

We are at Subi Samuel's studio which has been transformed into the lair of the Catwoman, who with a crack of a whip has everyone running around her succumbing to her every desire. The stunning looking Shilpa Shetty is practicing with a whip for her shoot in which her get up would inspire Tim Burton to make a Catwoman film and put Michelle Pfeiffer to shame. Subi is focused and his eye seems to be a shutter to the camera which is his world, as with a sharp look he looks at his muse before letting rip with his enigmatic image catcher.

"This is Shilpa's shoot, we're going for a different look," he informs me casually in between all the chaos swirling around me.

His assistants scurry all over the studio, raising lights and shifting backdrops all at the mental command of the ace photographer, as onlookers watch in amazement at poetry unfold before their eyes. Writers beware: inspiration overload. Subi is not a point and click man, his work is his life and art, and with careful precision he steals moments from reality immortalising them in his photographs to live on forever in the minds of whoever is fortunate enough to see them.

"Nikhil!" he bellows as a reflector is not held at the right angle for his model to be lit exactly how he wishes, and promptly his right hand boy gulps and changes the angle. 'Genius at Work' is what the door should read, yet to capture in words what magic Subi weaves would be to limit an art and so this report will have to suffice.

Shilpa pouts her lips and pierces with her eyes as the camera screams with a click and lights flash announcing a captured moment courtesy of the beautiful Shetty who knows her job to the hilt, and magician Subi. Media frenzy is a phrase which comes to mind with all the flashbulbs and clicks taking place but this shoot is for a sensitive looking man who quietly stands behind the action and watches his magazine covers be created, occasionally nodding approvingly.

Designer Reza watches carefully as his black skin tight catsuit creation envelopes Shilpa's body and is given life before his eyes, in between his running forward and adding to the shoot. If one was to plant a thousand seeds of imagination and leave them to grow the result would be Reza, whose name is pronounced 'razor' suited to his sharp eye for detail and amazing creations which cut through the conventional like a hot knife through butter.

"She's looking mind-blowing," Subi says as he breathes a sigh of relief in between the first costume change. "This is the look I wanted," he continues flashing the trademark Subi-smile at me, with a sparkle in his eye.

Minutes pass and Shilpa casually walks out without the cat's hood and clicks some close ups which look breathtaking in reality, one wonders how much they can be bettered on paper.
Everyone watches in awe, their jaws on the ground as Shilpa stuns to the extent that everyone's eyes are transfixed in a continuous gaze on her. Clicks later, it's time for the next change, and Subi orders the new backdrop to be put up and the lights changed. He attends to a few calls as his eyes haphazardly reflect his random inspirations which we will witness in the next few minutes.

I take this opportunity to corner Reza Shariffi, the man who has created and designed the catsuit for Shilpa as well as many other creations here today, and he happily talks of his work with as much passion as anyone who has an infinite enthusiasm for his art.

"Shilpa's catsuit is for a fantasy sequence for a magazine and she wanted to be a catwoman, which made me really happy because she is the perfect person and has the perfect body to fit into a catsuit. It was very easy body-wise to make the outfit for her because it fits her like a glove and is body-hugging suit. You can see the results!" he says with a smile as we prepare for her next entry which like a phaser, is set on stun.

Shilpa walks in wearing silver hot pants and a matching top, standing in front of the grunge-green background. As Subi takes his place after describing a pose she breaks into a barrage of poses, each one pleasing Subi's eye causing him to scream ecstatic praises her way in turn evoking more striking poses surpassing the last.

My eyes scan the room as everyone is either running around preparing the next shot or staring at the photographer and the person he is capturing, wanting to understand how their world works and how they have co-ordinated a perfect complementation. The final change occurs and a gold corset covers Shilpa along with blue denims, with her hair flashing hoped gold earrings in giggling snatches. Her smile commands attention and her beauty stands bold as Subi's shutter slices through time, imprisoning nano-seconds onto rolls of film.

She knows her job as does he, causing an unnerving anticipation for all of us waiting to witness the first peep at his masterpieces and wondering how dream pictures are painted through this killer combination.

Clicks fly and shutters slam before the final kill is made and the shoot is canned close to how the master wishes it to be.

"Pack up," he casually announces, staring deep within my eyes searching for a reaction to his shoot, before calling on his assistants to transform his studio back to normal. An empty space with a bookshelf in one corner and candles on the other, music dancing in the air and a wide open space where moments ago timeless art was created. The sounds simmer to silence and the bright bulbs fade to black as you realise what creations have just been born. The following minutes are just enough to allow the world to return to its usual rotation before he sets off again like a lit firecracker.

Expect the unexpected, forget all you know: You've just witnessed a shoot courtesy of Subi Samuel.

Fuad Omar

UNBREAKABLE: SHILPA SHETTY

There are those in this world who are born survivors despite whatever obstacles life will throw their way. Some of these people are subjected to the worst kind of torture and still shine through unscathed and braver, sporting a smile which hides a million tears. It is these people who become pioneers in their fields, are strong in character and commonly mentioned as inspirations to many. On seeing the tall, wide eyed dazzling beauty you'd never guess it, but Shilpa Shetty is one of these people who has endured more than her fair share of bad experiences.

My first meeting with her is at one of her photoshoots with Subi Samuel where she courteously offers me a handshake and a smile, before allowing me to witness the dedication and hard work she puts in to all she does which make her one of today's leading actresses of Indian cinema. She gives her all to the shoot which ensues making suggestions, mesmerizing the camera and oozing with determination yet carrying off effortlessly some of the most intricate shots, given the attire she has been asked to wear. A few hours later after basking in the Shetty magic, I discover the person behind the concocted media image and am proud to present to you a no-holds-barred honest look at the real Shilpa Shetty.

For those expecting someone even close to the person they've read about in filmi gossip magazines – prepare for disappointment.

I begin by asking about the first time she faced the camera as this is our first meeting and should begin at the beginning. She fixes me with her deep brown eyes as she speaks, and for those who have never had the pleasure of meeting Shilpa, I assure you she has eyes which beam like beacons of light, with every blink leaving you longing to drown deeper.

"I was modeling before I joined the film industry so I faced the camera before joining movies," she says confidently. "The first time I was modeling was for Limca so that was the first time I faced the camera. There's a lot of difference between the two mediums as with ad films the makers are extreme perfectionists, not to say that filmmakers aren't, but the emphasis is more on the product whereas in the film industry you are the product," she says with a laugh. Shilpa has literally been used as a product because her star status has meant she is seen as a public commodity and the same way that a political campaigner would hark and rave about issues to do with the country, the film journalists choose to shout about her, but unfortunately not always in a fair manner as will be revealed.

Sipping once more from those intoxicating eyes, I ask her about the road which began with Baazigar and being a supporting actress, led to being a glamour girl at times when cinema was losing meaning to evolving into a fully fledged and appreciated actress with her most recent venture Dhadkan, where finally she was given the opportunity to realise her potential.
"It's been rocky journey, but I've reached half way better late than ever. There's still a long way to go. I've been able to break the glamorous image people have labeled me with

and am being taken more seriously now because I've been fortunate enough to work with Dharmesh Dharshan. The kind of films I'm doing now are definitely different and the emphasis is on giving good performance rather than looking good."

I sense a feel of discontentment as for anyone with talent who is not allowed to express it to its fullest, it must be frustrating to have to go through so many films and not be allowed scope to give a fully fledged acting role which showcases your abilities. She agrees, but justifies that in her case,
"I never thought I'd last out this long because I never thought I'd make this into a prospective career. I was offered my first film while I was studying and also working at the time and that was a condition my father put forward that if I was going to foray into films I wouldn't quit my studies. Somewhere along the line once the outdoors started it was difficult to keep up with the syllabus and so I spoke to Dad and said 'If I'm working let me put my heart and soul into this because this is what I really enjoy,' and he understood."

Shilpa is someone who has evolved on screen before our eyes. At a time when films with little substance were coming out, she took the bold step of appearing in good films with an item number where she'd only be on screen to perform a song. This admirable move worked and she remained in the public eye and the hunger to see her on screen for a full film grew resulting in a fan following which grows by the day. She describes the risky move she took by being associated with songs rather than movies.
"Some in the film industry thought it was a wrong move for me, but I only did one item song in Shool, and I've

been very lucky with songs. Tarkieb and Jung just happened to have 'Dupatta ka Paloo' and 'Aila Re' which became very popular, and I had roles in those films too, they weren't just item numbers. These songs gained me popularity with children and it was a conscious move made by me as I thought I was out of people's minds and I did it and don't regret it." None of her fans regret it either as she's given some of the past few years' greatest musical hits which every filmgoer has danced to at some point or other. And as far as the suggestion that she could be out of people's minds anymore, the thought can be described as a now-near impossible task as her fan following proves.

Shilpa has a universal appeal and look missing in most of today's actresses. I remember reading an interview with legendary scriptwriter Salim Khan who said he could see Shilpa in the guise of Phoolan Devi as she has a powerful presence which cannot be ignored. Her appeal crosses over the generations and she also has a large following among the very young as well as teenagers and young adults.
"I believe the only way you can become really popular is with children. If they like you and love you, you know you'll be around for a while," she says with a spark in her eyes reflecting an obvious deep love for children.
"Children loved me in Baazigar and the feedback I got thereafter was like people telling me that after seeing Chura Ke Dil Mera my daughter forced me to buy the same leopard print skirt you were wearing in the song, when I did Shool it was the way I raised my eyebrows, it's amazing how these little things go a long way! I really like being popular among children in comparison to being the sex symbol because children are so pure and innocent they just like you from the heart."

Asking her to pick any favourite films or roles she takes me on a ride through her career and in her case the standard line is true – it is too difficult to choose a favourite given each film for her has literally pushed her forward and to the next stage. She shows a true love for her art as she talks of the milestones in her career fondly.

"Each of my films is like my own babies, and I've learned so much from each one. Each experience has helped me evolve as an actress and I've learnt from both the good and bad ones. Baazigar was my introduction, Chura Ke Dil Mera was a milestone in my career and Shool was a good move for me. Jung was a film where the only thing people talked about of the film was my song and Dhadkan was like a new lease of life so it's very difficult to pick and choose any favourites, but it's definitely been a well travelled journey."

Dhadkan is like a new debut for Shilpa. When she arrived on the scene she was given a good supporting role but then Indian cinema went back to the time-tested formula of having male-oriented central characters leaving the actress in the film to merely add glamour to the movie. Her journey is certainly well travelled as finally she has been given a deserved opportunity, and this is only the beginning of her career as up until now she has only been allowed to survive. Survival is the key word judging by the media in India. Shilpa has been a victim of the gossip magazines and experienced a level of press attention which can only reaffirm her importance and the need for the media to rip apart those they see as good people. In her case there was no need for them to put her up on a pedestal, for she already stood there as a good human being, so they chose to defame her in every way possible flexing their self-obsessed biceps in an attempt to show her their power.

"I've never been media savvy or believed that any publicity is good publicity as the saying goes. I'm come from a very secure background and what only really matters to me is my work and my family and not how good my PR is. Very recently I took a stand against Stardust," (a film magazine in India which nests neatly between a cross between the National Enquirer and the Sun), "because what they were writing was really below the belt and sometimes silence is misunderstood and you have to draw the line. So I said if the truth is on my side I have to stand up and fight for it and the only way I could do this was in court, so we've managed to pass an injunction on a big publication like this which is the first time it's gotten this far. They took me for granted which is not a very good thing and before that I don't think anyone had written anything so nasty about me. But I guess it's all a part of life and somewhere I've learnt from this experience and they've also learnt a lesson."

There's a sense of sadness in her eyes, not belonging to the step she's taken but associated to the hurt she has endured because of the media who preyed on her like a pack of wolves and undeservedly maligned her character in a ruthless and unforgiving manner, peppering every story with the result of an overactive and vile imagination. I look into her eyes which shine like pools of light, every ripple being affected by the character assassination she has been subjected to and send a silent prayer for this charmingly sweet young woman and her family to be shielded from such inhuman atrocities from hereafter.

Her fan following increases by the hour and it seems the media always chooses the most-loved celebrities to make their scapegoat, as proves the kind of fanmail she receives.

"A lot of children write into me and want to make me their sister or a part of their family," she begins as I smile wondering how anyone could resist making the ethereal and bubbly beauty a part of their lives, as her genuineness shines through in a world of false entities. Lost in her words I gaze on as she continues.

"Girls write to me empathising with characters I play such as in Dhadkan because in India they would still give up their lovers for their parents because that's the way they've been brought up. I guess a lot of girls identified with that character and it made an impact."

Her fans hail her as a role model, so I have to ask who has inspired her the most, and her answer reveals an all Indian heart, filled with warmth and affection for those who have stood by her.

"It would have to be my family. I went through a low phase just before Dhadkan when there came a time when a certain producer even removed me from his film, and I felt like giving it all up and I asked my Mom why am I going through this, why am I putting up with it? There's no reason for me to take this and I didn't want all the pressure of trying to be someone else when I was happy being who I am. She saw what I went through and saw me through it saying 'After night there is always day, and this is only a passing phase and what happens is for the best because if you don't experience a low phase you won't value success'."

Words to the wise as nothing can truly be appreciated until one understands what it is like in its absence. I can only imagine what it would be like to have such a saviour at a time when all seemed lost. As she continues, my question is answered.

"She was so right, because when Dhadkan was released and went on to become a hit I really valued it. I never took things lightly because I've worked hard for every success I've got and for every film I've done. When Mom said that to me I joined the gym, I worked on my look, my make up and my clothes. I searched for wherever there could've been something lacking and tried my best at everything and it showed. I love changing the way I look and try not to look the same in any two films or photos, and I think if it wasn't for my parents I would've given up long ago. They've always been there like a pillar of strength and support."

As she tells me all this my mind is cast back to when I first met her mother and how I still remember the hospitality and warmth with which she welcomed me, and if one thing I know for a fact and is reiterated by Shilpa's experience is that the Shettys are a very warm and loving family, close to each other in every way and supportive in all they do. One only needs to look at what Shilpa has been through to see her strength of character, to understand an ounce of her pain and talk to her to see the way her eyes glow whenever her mother is mentioned and the sincere heartfelt affection she has with the family she bonds with so very closely.

Before we end the interview she leaves me with more words from her experiences, hoping to provide encouragement for anyone who has dreamt a dream and wished it to come true. It is amazing to find someone so young full of such experiences but I guess it's true what they say about a person is not as old as their age dictates, but as mature as experience has taught them.

"If you have a dream, you can see it come true. All you have to is believe in it and work towards it. I'm living proof of it. I was really thin and gawky, never won any competitions in my school and wanted to do catwalk modeling. I went to a leading ramp choreographer when I was 17 and she told me I was too thin, too short and didn't know how to walk. A few years later Chura Ke Dil Mera became a rage and I was being introduced as the girl with the fabulous walk! It was really ironic as I was chief guest at a modeling function where that same choreographer was present and it was just proof that whatever you go through happens for the best, God had something better in store for me. Every incident that has occurred in my life, if God has taken away from me He's given back to me tenfold more. I want people to know and believe that if they don't have something today and they want it just work towards it, believe in God and it will happen. It will happen!"

She smiles as she gives me a quote which will give birth to a new generation of survivors and ambitious hard workers, and she proves the reason she is quoted by many as being someone who is a source of inspiration. Her words resonate with sincerity and her eyes penetrate deep as though she is talking to my soul, planting the seed of good wishes and positivity in me as a gift from her.

There are people on this earth who are born survivors and truly inspire. Today I not only got to meet the real Shilpa Shetty as opposed to the fabricated image created by media circles with vested interests, but also got to hear the story of a survivor. The highlight of our meeting was not witnessing the photoshoot or being with the brown-eyed beauty, but being able to sit and talk to someone who has made me feel…truly inspired.

Fuad Omar

AFTAB SHIVDASANI: THE FLASH

Aftab Shivdasani is coming your way faster than The Flash. Like a non-stop locomotive, the young actor is about to bamboozle your senses like never before. You won't know what hit you. You won't know whether to laugh or cry, because he's about to make you do both. With an impressive line up of releases which showcase the young man's talent, he is all set to rock your Summer and he has no regrets. Ladies and gentleman, presenting the king chameleon himself, Aftab Shivdasani.

The interview with Aftab has been one talked about and co-ordinated for a while, but we somehow keep missing each other. By chance, on visiting a friend I'm told "Aftab's here!" with a smile, and so I walk into the studio, and there he is, standing tall, slightly bulky from his gym workouts and turning to see who's entered, swinging his head round like a creeping camera shot which highlights a heroine's zulfey in slow motion. I say his name and walk towards him as he greets me with a handshake and a smile, and we instantly know who the other is. Moments later I feel as though I'm in the company of an old friend and we're chatting to the 9's about everything and anything.

Eyeing the time and not wanting this opportunity to slip by, I click record and launch into the interview.

We begin by entering the time tunnel, travelling back to when Aftab entered the industry with Ramgopal Verma's

Mast, an impressive launch vehicle that didn't exactly achieve huge success but gained its young debutante a loyal fan following that mobbed him wherever he went. I ask the young bundle of energy to wax lyrical about how it felt being acknowledged and embraced as an actor, even though the film was not.

"It's extremely encouraging because you know that even though the film was not as appreciated as you'd hoped, at least you were appreciated as a person. I came on my own two feet, had no backing or support and made it totally on my own and then to be accepted is wonderful. I had a pretty impressive debut but even though the film didn't do well I was still picked up by other filmmakers who still had faith in me and a huge fan following too, so it felt and still feels pretty good!" he says in between breaths, unable to contain his excitement as he recalls those days.

"It feels amazing because it gives you the motivation that you need and the encouragement that you are still right there and are being looked up to and appreciated, it's a very warm feeling."

Being a newcomer and not a star son, nor someone who's experience in the industry was paramount, I ask what the learning experience was like while making Mast and what making the film taught him.

"I learnt that acting came naturally to me, because essentially acting is within you. And no one can teach you how to act. Something must be there for you to be able to act, and acting classes and schools make you shed all your inhibitions but cannot make you act. They can only make you more comfortable and more prepared for the camera.

So acting is something that has to come from inside you, and to date I've never taken any acting classes or anything but I've always been pretty comfortable in front of the camera."

And pretty comfortable is putting it mildly. Whether he's the fresh faced college Romeo in search of his silver screen Juliet in Mast, the ruthless newspaper editor of Kasoor who's terrifying us or the guy who smiles cheekily while trying to get the girl in the promos of Pyar, Ishq aur Mohabbat, Aftab certainly makes an impact when on screen.
But before this confident and plucky Aftab was evident, he was still a learning fresher and he continues about one of his most important lessons from the failure of Mast.

"Mast was my first venture in front of the camera as an actor, and its failure taught me a lot. Its helped me grow as a human being and accept failure. Having a taste of failure helps prepare you for the rest of the journey. Success is just a delay of failure so you have to take both in your stride, and can't take either one too seriously," he says laughing inbetwixt turning slightly philosophical.

From seeing failure with Mast, but acceptance, and now seeing success with Kasoor and the promising response of Love Ke Liye Kuch Bhi Karega, a nurtured love from fans, I ask him to reminisce and describe his journey.
"It feels like I've grown up from a child to a man. The whole journey has been so beautiful because the entire making of Mast was a dream and a complete learning process," he says looking back.

"The first shot I gave I wasn't nervous because I'd been in front of the camera before, but it was my first time as the lead, as the 'hero'. The whole unit from the technicians to my co-stars all made me feel comfortable and it was a very warm atmosphere, and even though I never actually had any nervousness or anxiety it was still very encouraging to have this environment which nurtures and edges you on. So from then I've grown up a lot and now I can't live without working!"

Hello? Faced the camera before? Yes dear readers, the Aftab that was introduced to the international arena through Mast is India's own Truman Burbank, and has grown up knowing less the television screen and more the camera lens.

"I started out as the Farex baby when I was 14 months old so then after a gap of five years at the age of six onwards I was doing commercial ads up until the age of 19. Then because of my ad films I got Mast, which was my debut film. Ramgopal Verma saw my work and screen tested me and the rest is history!" he informs me, letting me in on how the cherubic heartthrob first faced the camera when he a little tot.

'What?' I gasp. No struggling?

He smiles the midas smile and says:
"I had to struggle in terms of getting work, but never to get a break, it was God's grace. It's all destiny and whatever is coming your way will find its way to you, in fact it's funny you're here interviewing me for the UK because I was going to come to London to do my MBA after graduating!"

Hmmm. The wonderkid in London, loafing around Leicester Square and skipping classes at Cambridge, I can see how the thought would entertain many of his UK fans as they are probably reading this and screaming that he could have been in their class. He reads my mind and laughs loud. I try to compose myself and remember this is an interview, which is difficult given how much a barrel of fun the new kid on the block is.

I remind him of the alternate route to London being stage shows and given this year we've seen somewhat of an absence of them, I'm sure his UK fan following can tempt him to dance his way to Wembley arena.
The smile returns and nodding his head he says:
"I'll come for shows once I have a little more credit to my name, I want to do a bit better first. I'll have six releases up until August so people are going to get fed up of me!"

Hang on, I think. Mast was quite a wee while back and Kasoor marked a kindred return to the big screen didn't it? So how could those fans be fed up of him, he's only resurfaced after ages.

"Almost a year and a half after my first film, I'm back on the big screen. There was a big gap between Mast and Kasoor, so all my patient, loving fans who have been waiting to see me since Mast, you'll be seeing a lot more of me in the coming months and hopefully I can come to London soon and meet my fans and catch up with them," he says, charming my readers with the Pyar Ishq aur Mohabbat look in his eyes.

"After Kasoor my next is a film for Ramgopal Verma which came out recently called Love Ke Liye Kuch Bhi

Karega which is a hilarious and again in total contrast to both Mast and Kasoor. I play a really, really funny guy and it's so difficult to shoot because we're just always laughing on the sets! That's a film I've been really looking forward to. Then is Rajiv Rai's movie called Pyar Ishq Mohabbat which was shot in Scotland and Switzerland more than anywhere else. It's about three guys after one girl but despite the rumours it's not like There's Something About Mary. I have a film for Mr Boney Kapoor which has Esha Deol and myself in the film called Koi Mere Dil Se Poochey. That's a mainstream commercial film with romance and action which is shaping up pretty well. Then I'm doing an out-and-out romantic film for Tips which is with Amisha Patel and then there's another one with Amisha also which is more a comedy type movie for the masses and the classes. So I've got a completely diversified variety of roles for people to look forward to seeing me in!"

Those who have been following the circuit will now have been awaiting Pyar Ishq aur Mohabbat with baited breath. The promos have been received very well and in the UK the music is booming out on the Broadway, with kids hanging around the Southall stalls mimicking his finger point and shaky walk we witness on the green as he goes towards Keerti Reddy singing "..qayamat ho jaata hai..". With the ads of Love Ke Liye Kuch Bhi Karega promising a riot of a comedy, especially Aftab and Fardeen's comic mannerisms and hilarious expressions, alongside the increasingly popular 'Aslam Bhai' number, it seems the world is ready to fall in love with Aftab again. And I'm sure he doesn't have a problem with that.

With so much lined up and so many different roles for his fans to look forward to, I ask what's left that he wants to do, and if any role exists he hasn't played and is dying to sink his teeth into.

"I'd love to do an action movie," he says responding almost immediately.

"One which has hard hitting action with a tinge of romance so you feel for the character and believe in what you're seeing. Action is my favourite genre and I love films like Predator and Braveheart, I love watching Nicholas Cage and Arnold, so I want to try my hand at a good action movie and prove I'm good at both romance and action."

Aftab packing a punch with his fists as well as with his comedy and acting sounds like a tempting cocktail. Judging by his new improved physical stature, it seems he is already training for this foray into action and given how neatly he seems to slot into any role, he could just give the others a run for their money. Aftab is fortunate to not have been slotted in any particular genre as yet, and given what he's going to hit us with in the coming months it seems he won't allow anyone to label him. Except with one term: actor.

The response to his promos, posters and the recent poll which revealed a majority of UK fans will be seeing Pyar Ishq aur Mohabbat mostly for him, then the music and then Arjun Rampal, it seems he cannot escape public adoration. If I was a betting man, I know where my money would be.

I eye the time once more and begin to wrap up, asking Aftab to leave a message for those who have watched, supported and are rooting for him, be it in India or in the UK, or anywhere. What would he like to say to them. He stops to think before answering. Taking a deep breath, he holds the tape recorder and looks down.

His words resonate with heartfelt thanks as he says:
"Despite my first film not doing well I have been given so many opportunities and it's thanks to the blessings of those who have supported me and wished me well, so please tell them I love them and it's because of them I'm here standing on my own two feet, and I'm going to fight and struggle until I've achieved the kind of success I'm looking forward to and I will never ever let them down."

Given the wheels he's put into motion, the last thing he can do is let anyone down. Varied roles, top filmmakers and a promise to keep the flame burning as long as that spark is in his eye, hungry for good work and different roles. Interviewing Aftab is like walking in and talking to a friend who's passionate about cinema and what he does, with many laughs thrown in for good measure. His down to earth attitude and ambition, combined with a killer instinct will only help him achieve his dreams. Aftab Shivadasani is heading your way. In many guises, in various forms. Prepare your senses for an onslaught of entertainment: You have been warned.

Fuad Omar

THE ELUSIVE INTERVIEW

Writing about Aishwarya Rai is easy, it's interviewing her that's difficult. Not for the reasons many would have you believe of starry tantrums, aloofness or impossible co-ordinations, but for another reason that to many editors, press agents and fans makes no sense whatsoever.

I was recently asked to interview Aishwarya for the 'Making of' one of her forthcoming films before her accident, and after a slight hesitation I declined and said it would be better if someone else did it, but I'd write the questions if the need arose. Three years ago, it was actually a mission I aimed to accomplish: I wanted to sit her down and ask her everything I had ever wondered about her preparation for roles, her performances and the way in which she manages to remain all smiles despite a gruelling and torturous schedule. Last year when I was assigned to mentor a then up and coming journalist one piece of advice I departed on her was to interview people as early on in communication as possible, because you should write about what fascinates you and the people that interest you, and to not take it for granted that permission for an interview meant they would bare their soul either, the real skill and a journalist's job is to extract information from their interviewee that nobody else would think of, not be given information on a platter. Today Aishwarya Rai still fascinates me, probably more so than before I met her. Every few weeks or few months she'll pull off something that is not only a leap forward for her as an actress but she'll manage to do something you'll never hear about but will touch someone's heart and make them smile for months on end. Initially what rattled me was the constant attention given to her looks at the expense of her talent and hard work. If anyone wants to praise her beauty please do, but that's not a part of her she's worked hard to accomplish but a gift from God and her parents. Her hard work, dedication to her profession and refusal to settle for anything other than the best from herself, now that's something to really applaud and talk about. I still get chills watching Hum Dil De Chuke Sanam when she lets out a gut-wrenching shriek telling her mother how the man she loves has touched her spirit and soul like no-one before, her performance is not only spell-binding it's sheer magic. She holds that film together and to date I joke that it is her most violent film because she completely massacres the audience's emotions throughout. I could write a whole piece on Hum Dil De Chuke Sanam and its camerawork, the performances, Sanjay Leela Bhansali's direction and the choreography, but to get stuck in a moment is to let the world pass you by, and Aishwarya has never allowed that to happen.

With Devdas, yet again Aishwarya is finally getting overdue credit in the form of recognition for her talent, hard work and professionalism in comparison to earlier when these efforts were eclipsed by her looks, which some scribes could not get past to see the girl who slowly but swiftly climbed the ladder to become the actress she is today. She worked to painful extremes to perfect her dancing and the blisters on display on her feet during the shooting of HDDC testify to the fact she is nothing short of a perfectionist. She went on to further torture her feet with Taal and then embark on a world tour with Aamir and Akshaye where she dazzled everyone. Many came to catch a glimpse of her, but went away even more satisfied and surprised the beauty had such thunderous dance performances in the HDDCS and Taal dance sequences as well as the tribute to Indian cinema medley where she came on stage through many changes enacting, emoting and enchanting.

Her next opportunity to make a real mark came in Aditya Chopra's Mohabbatein where she executed a role so well you could work backwards and write the character onto paper because it required a presence with etched out nuances that had to be discovered, not defined. I personally feel her performance in the film is completely underrated but with time will be heralded as will Shah Rukh's because it is a film quite like no other. The next period of her career has been one where she was questioned and put into the limelight and never for professional reasons, but personal. Speculation, rumours and gossip concerning Aishwarya somehow qualified as front page news eclipsing factual stories since succumbing to sensationalism resulted in sales, with the only casualty as far as the media were concerned being Aishwarya's image. But the silent, resilient personality answered every story and rumour through biding her time, she didn't want to grab headlines any way she could, but be noted for her contribution to cinema and not to the gossip columns. Hard work paid off as she delivered in the cinematic masterpiece that is Devdas, where she mesmerised as Paro and came up with a multi-award winning performance and recognised achievement through showing that a HDDCS was no fluke, but a teaser for what was to come. I've been warned not to write too much about Devdas given the reams I penned on the film, Shah Rukh's performance and Aishwarya's performance throughout 2002, but I will reiterate that in it she proved yet again her versatility as an actress, ability to perform a much quieter character who revealed more with her eyes and look, her body language and demeanour than the simple and straightforward Nandini of HDDCS. For anyone who questioned her talent before, they will not get the opportunity again. She swept the awards and deservedly so, but unfortunately she's been in the news for all the wrong reasons because cinematic achievements somehow seem to be avoided by the so-called film press and personal losses or rumours tend to dominate columns and front pages.

Following the success of HDDCS and Devdas and the fact that their success can be majorly attributed to Aishwarya, her contribution to cinema could no longer be questioned; on stage she was magic, on screen a goddess, and a firebrand in taking on any role be it comedic, emotionally intense or romantic. She consolidated her international position further through delivering Dil Ka Rishta which topped the UK and US charts and even broke box office records in South Africa.

Aishwarya Rai has this year not only dominated Indian cinema awards but Indian cinema itself. I'm extremely excited about Rituparno Ghosh's Choker Bali in which the actress has a sans-make up look and is the most illuminating you'll ever see her on screen. She's shot the film in Bengali completely and dedicated all she can to making the filmmaker's vision a reality.

"We got along fabulously," says Ghosh, "and I convinced her to wipe off all makeup and wear a completely natural look for Choker Bali (meaning, a girl who's an eyesore). But the irony is that she's hardly that! I don't think Ash has ever looked better."

The film is based on Rabindranath Tagore's acclaimed novel of the same title, and has Aishwarya playing a young widow, Binodini, who is torn between her two suitors in the conservative society of Bengal about 100 years ago. It's a great challenge for any actress and one Aishwarya Rai has taken head on and given her all to. With international offers regularly pouring in her direction, the fact that she's the international face of brands such as Longines and L'Oreal and is now the first Indian to be part of the auspicious Cannes jury which recognises achievement, Aishwarya's journey is just beginning. The films she has lined up are no small features – Rohan Sippy's Kuch Naa Kaho is a film where she's effortlessly portrayed as complex a relationship as life throws at you and Choker Bali is by the combination of director and actress alone, exceptional. Bride and Prejudice is Gurinder Chadha's offering which allows Santosh Sivan to present Aishwarya as never before and you can bet if he shoots her at twilight or during 'magic hour' it will be a moment not to be missed, so what she has to offer still is as exciting as what's come to pass.

So if Aishwarya is someone who continues to fascinate me on the basis of her expanding and exciting projects (so much so that it's so easy to write like this *about* her) then why is it so difficult to interview her? It's not an easy question to answer but I think deep down I'd rather enjoy the positive experiences she goes through as an observer, as a friend and as a writer who becomes inspired by her work and experiences and who she is, than sit and interview a friend. I make it a point to do one definitive interview with every actor I feel has contributed to Indian cinema in such an enormous manner that it needs to be documented as representation that this is what this person contributed to cinema during this period of time, so I guess it's just a matter of time until interviewing Aishwarya is a reality I'm going to have to face because already she's making history and has etched her name clearly into the books. But I think when that day comes, it really will be a truly legendary piece that will aim to capture the essence of all she encompasses and has given to her craft in one long interview because her journey is one only seen as a scratch on the surface if what comes in print is anything to go by, because the real truth and her own journey of discovery, triumph and mastery of her art is truly inspiring.

Aishwarya Rai is no longer thought of as the young girl who conquered the world in 1994 and made Indians proud on one eventful evening, she's seen as an icon of today who makes so many so proud every single day and is conquering the world all over again. It's an exciting time to be Aishwarya Rai, but it's even more exciting a time to be a film fan. This is just the beginning…

Fuad Omar

Aishwarya Rai, live on stage at Wembley in 1999

ANDAAZ: PRESS JUNKET

Ever wondered what a Bollywood press junket is like? Well accept this invite and listen up!

Andaaz had its press launch a few weeks ago and it was an insanely hectic weekend, (as you'd expect otherwise it wouldn't be a successful one). What began at 530 in the morning on Friday as I struggled to keep my eyes open on the way to picking up Akshay Kumar, ends as I type this and not a second before.

Akshay's plane was slightly delayed and it took the Khiladi king a little more time than expected to come out of the airport due to the rush with producer Suneel Darshan keen to present his film to the UK and introduce his stars. Due to the delay at the busy airport we had a few minutes to get somewhere else to pick up Priyanka Chopra and Lara Dutta. However, at any time of morning it's a pleasure to see the two chirpy girls especially if they're greeting you with smiles galore and conversation.

"How you doing?" says Priyanka with a smile as try our best to get to the car as soon as possible, and Lara and I exchange conversation about her forthcoming films namely Andaaz and Mumbai Se Aaya Mera Dost, both of which I've heard a lot about from common friends and her co-stars.

Whisking away towards the hotel, time flies through mentally making a note of how busy a day lies before us and at what time the trio are seeing who. Arriving at the hotel and sorting out rooms and a conference room takes no time, dealing with press waiting for interviews takes a lot of time and talking to people who seem to serve no purpose other than to confuse you is, well confusing.

Priyanka breathes a sigh of relief as she spies the bed. "Do we get time to rest?" she asks, her eyes hopeful and smile aiming to charm a yes out of the team that's brought her here. There's no such luck but a few stolen moments are arranged for all three to freshen up before the mayhem begins.

I first met Priyanka in India, a few months after she took the Miss World crown and the first thing that struck me about her was her charisma and personality. She has great courage of her every word and is not only exceptionally well spoken but an intelligent and thoughtful person. She can mimic a British accent perfectly and always has the same aura around her every time we meet, and that's one of positivity. I last met her a few months ago in India where she had just finished another Andaaz photo shoot with Lara and Akshay and was heading off, and at that time we had no idea she'd be in London now, but then again one of the first things I thought when meeting her after Miss World in India was 'what is she doing in India??'!

Suneel Darshan is an extremely busy man. This is his production and he's also the one responsible for recent UK successes such as Ek Rishta and Haan Maine Bhi Pyaar Kiya as well as Talaash. Yet he takes time out to talk to everyone and brief them on how he'd like his latest venture to be portrayed. The bustling has begun and Akshay is ready before you know it. I swear he's mastered some cosmic mojo that fuels his martial arts and discipline – throughout his UK stay he was ultra-efficient and the first to be everywhere. At the press conference someone asked me what I thought the chances of Andaaz's success were and I answered with complete honesty that I only knew the creative team behind the film was a good one and so believed in the project. I elaborated later in a radio interview at how Akshay is someone who has been in the industry for a long time and overcome every obstacle put before him and answered every detractor to survive and be where he is today. For him to have such international successes and have completely taken on the variety of roles he's undertaken is no easy feat. The hard work has paid off and the superstar is where he is today – launching two new actresses and still looking the same he did a decade ago. He's happily married, has a gorgeous son and is flying as high as his character in Andaaz, except he's doing it without a plane.

It's almost 11 and the video interviews are supposed to have begun, but the girls aren't ready given the delay in getting to the hotel. Posters are being put up and cut-outs dragged along to transform the Washington Mayfair's conference room into a mini Bollywood auditorium.

"I saw a glimpse of Lara," says someone who has turned up but is not press, "she's gorgeous!". I make a mental note to pass on the compliment to her later but for now there's more pressing matters at hand. The press have started arriving and Akshay is the only one completely ready. Nadeem looking suave and sophisticated strolls in and is ready to face the questions, a mini-swarm of music journalists have come especially to meet him. Up inside the room Priyanka and Lara are ready and a photographer who has been promised a photo shoot begins clicking away. The swarm closes in as my mobile beeps every two minutes in between shouting how fantastic the shots are, the photographers downstairs are eager to get their photos too.

"I'm shooting for a whole lot of films," says Priyanka justifying how hectic her life is at the moment. "It seems that the industry liked my performance in The Hero, and the response to Andaaz so far has been positive. All in all, I am very excited".

Lara is someone you'd easily confused with being British too because of the accent, and she has a smile that just lights up the room every time. In Andaaz she has a pivotal role that allows her to showcase her acting talent and in Mumbai Se Aaya Mera Dost opposite Abhishek she is looking stunning in a very different film that promises to be a scorcher.

"I picked my scripts carefully from the ones that came my way. I couldn't have hoped for a better producer than Suneel Darshan or a better director than Raj Kanwar. They have been in the business long enough to know what the audience wants without getting crass about it. I had an amazing experience working on Andaaz. It was almost like being part of the family. Being an untrained actress, I have my own method of acting which works for me."

It's almost showtime. The photographers want a photo session outside and some people nobody recognises as being part of the guest list have ambled into the conference room, and we make a mutual decision to let them be. Since it's not raining and the three stars don't mind, they are led outside and the cameras click away. Suneel Darshan looks on with pride at his find, the coming together of the superstar and two beauty queens is his doing, and that too in a film with a different treatment of a lover from the past meeting the lover of the present. I thought about this before today and it's certainly a frightening concept. What if you loved someone so much and knew they were right for you but couldn't be with them, and so while getting over them fell into another relationship only to have the love of the past return into your life? What happens? Check out Andaaz when it releases in May, but for now it's time to break up the cameras and ask the stars to come inside.

I introduce the team one by one and each is greeted with a round of applause and since we're running slightly late we begin a Q and A session instantly. An hour later and all questions asked, it's time for the tougher part to begin – getting the stars away from the press (especially those who choose not to ask anything in the open press conference but rush forward to meet them immediately after for an autograph or photo), and upstairs for a photo-shoot. It happens, slowly but surely. After the shoot as we exit there's a small gathering of journalists we have to breeze by with somewhere else to be and then a few more hectic moments later it's time to head to the BBC.

On the way out again, Priyanka, Lara and Akshay stop to smile for the photographs and sign away proving how yet again it's not easy doing what they do as they landed early in the morning and haven't had a moment to stop since or eat or rest and are expected to be bright and enthusiastic wherever they go.
After a brief stint on CBBC on Bollywood, it's time to head off to Sunrise radio and take phone calls, then dinner and the end of day one. There must have been at least twenty interviews and over a hundred photographs and there's even more tomorrow. Who said doing a press junket was easy?

The Andaaz press conference was organised by Shree Krishna International in association with Tip Top Entertainment and myself. Andaaz is released on May 23rd.

Fuad Omar

Hosting the Andaaz press conference in July 2003 (top) and with Priyanka Chopra (below)

With Lara Dutta (above) and coverage in the Asian Xpress (below)

THREE-MENDOUS!

BOLLYWOOD'S leading beauties flew to the home of action hero James Bond this week, where they could soon be starring opposite 007 himself.

Ex Miss World Priyanka Chopra and former Miss Universe Lara Dutta are rumoured to be starring alongside Aishwarya Rai in the next Bond movie.

They arrived in London to meet adoring fans in a glittering event organised by Asian Xpress's Bollywood guru Fuad Omar.

Arriving in style with hunk Akshay Kumar by their side, the stars rolled up to the Washington Hotel in Mayfair where fans and a swarm of journalists were waiting to greet them. With music legend Nadeem accompanying the actors, it was an afternoon of questions and answers about their latest movie Andaaz and other hot topics.

For Akshay, there was no better time to get in the good books of his co-stars. "The girls have done an excellent job. It never felt like I was working with newcomers. When we shot the movie, their attitude and dedication showed from the very first instance. I think this is a fabulous launch for them," he gushed.

Looking glamorous as ever, beauty queen Lara Dutta was quick to defend why she had taken so long to hit Bollywood. "Once I got back after the year as Miss Universe, I was waiting for the right film, as I would be seen on screen for the first time. I also took time off to be with my family," she said.

Now all have their fingers crossed for their latest movie, Andaaz, which looks set to be a Bollywood blockbuster. The romance in the film revolves around Raj (Akshay Kumar) and Kajol (Lara Dutta) who have been best friends since childhood. Hoping to marry Kajol, Raj's hopes are soon dashed when she marries someone else. Jiya (Priyanka Chopra) soon arrives on the scene and more romance ensues.

AMRITA ARORA: BEFORE THE DAWN

Amrita Arora is about to be huge. Her debut film is almost ready for release and she's a bundle of positive energy, looking like a glowing light bulb rather than someone who should be tired after completing her first film. I first met her at a party where it was too dark to make out who exactly she was and the only impression I got was that she was rather short. Today when I meet Amrita Arora, I realise it must have been really dark at the party and she must have been sitting down. She welcomes me into the plush residence where family photos adorn the table tops and you're not allowed in unless you're smiling, because after you meet her you definitely will be.

Wearing a white tee and denims, with hair that looks ruffled, yet sits neatly below her shoulders like intertwined black and brown silken threads woven together to complement her beautiful face and deeply reflective eyes, she sits comfortably and offers me a drink to combat the rising temperature in the Mumbai heat. After exchanging a few words it's clear we are getting on like old friends and the Dictaphone runs as we chat to the nines about her journey to the place where she is today: sitting with a smile on the fence that has 'SUCCESS' painted on the other side, biding her time with glee.

Rather than ask the nymphet of niceness about her background and the rest, I felt from our brief conversation prior to hitting record she's done so much at such a young age that it's more a journey which has led her to where she is now, and this too is the end of one phase and the first step of another journey, so ask her to tell me when her achievements started, and she takes me on her travels with her as she beams that smile of hers and reminisces about her beginnings.

"It all started waaay back when I was in school and college," she says with a sparkle in her light brown eyes. "There have been achievements of sorts like winning debates, elocution and competing on an intercollegiate level, and when I started college I won the VJ Hunt, which is pretty big over here. They auditioned many people from Madras, Delhi, Calcutta and Mumbai and they had the final round here where they wanted to select four new people and introduce them onto MTV. There were hundreds of people who auditioned and I was lucky enough to come in the first twelve and even luckier to have finally won it. That's really where the story starts, and I was a VJ with MTV and that's where the journey began. It was really exciting and nice but overnight you're thrown into this situation where you have to survive and you meet a lot of people, travel and broaden your horizons. Then like any other girl in India, her sights are always set on the world of Bollywood!" she says barely able to contain her ecstatic enthusiasm.

"I guess it was a natural move for me," she continues, "because I was always getting a lot of offers and it was just a matter of timing for me and being in the right place at the right time. Mr Mehul Kumar was watching TV and was on the look out for a new girl for his film, and was looking for someone fresh and able to suit his character, doing justice to the role he wanted to portray and he saw me on MTV and wanted to meet me. I walked into the office, signed the film and we began shooting, almost have now completed the film and the rest is history! I left MTV and began a new journey, and it's been really fun, I've met a lot of people and the whole experience has been completely overwhelming."

Amrita is still smiling and it's becoming infectious. I can't help but feel happy for her and amazed at how fast and so young she has achieved so much, and so it's now my turn to beam at her and ask along this journey of the last few years, which have been her favourite stops.

"The wild times, masti, masala at college is definitely the first! Just what goes with being a teenager thrown into the whole college life scenario and trying to fit in, I love that! The next stop would be MTV because it was the first time I realised I really want to be successful in what was given to me, and I wanted to not only survive and be one of the many, but just be The One. That phase of my life that made me realise I had an identity of my own that was separate to being Malaika's sister or just being the sister-in-law to the reputed Khan family, it was a time I'd consider my calling or becoming. That was definitely one of my favourite stops."

The becoming of Amrita Arora. I like it. The moment of epiphany that dawns realisation as to where her destiny lies, and Amrita had found it, and that too at such an early age. Before I can wonder why my life has passed relatively slower than the Amrita Express train, she picks up my thoughts telepathically and says:

"And this stop wasn't really a stop because it's still going on, the rail-gaari is still chook-chooking right through my life!" she says letting out a burst of laughter.

By now she has me. I am totally immersed in her sweet charms and now know who to call for a dosage of happiness and laughter, should I start missing London too much. She moves on to telling me about how the journey has been a learning experience of not only modelling in front of the camera but also the way things work behind the camera, using the time to pick up new skills that she feels could better her now and in the future.

"It's been great because it's like traveling. While my friends are all still studying I'm moving from one place to another and I'm just enjoying it, it's like a high. It's like I've been given this opportunity and I just want to do the best I can."

She shifts in her chair as I take a breather from watching this girl literally grow in front of me through the journey she has narrated to me in the past half hour. Now she has reached another stop, I ask her to remember her very first shot for her movie, Kitne Door Kitne Paas, on hearing which, she bursts out laughing once again. Moments later, attempting to compose herself, she recounts the story of her first day shooting.

"My first day was a simple scene in a police station where all I had to do was react to my co-star Fardeen's dialogue, which was really easy. Now the next day we started filming a song, and you know how our songs are. There were loads of people and it suddenly hit me that 'here I am about to be on 70mm, shooting a film and this is really larger than life!' Now we were to shoot what is the most intimate moment of the song, and it scared the hell out of me. I was really embarrassed and had to do it in front of this janta, my producer and director and was just not getting it right, and they were really patient because after three takes I still wasn't getting it right. After the eighth take I was so upset that I ruined my make up because I was literally bawling thinking 'what is this, why is this happening!' and Fardeen was being really co operative and said let's ease off and give her some easy stuff to start with. But we pulled it off, because he spoke to me in a corner and said 'don't think of anyone out there and no one can do this like you, you're gonna be the best' and basically a pep talk, and it worked. I went out there and I kicked ass!"

As if on cue, she squeals into further reams of laughter and by now you can literally feel the positive vibe this girl has and how wonderfully happy she is.
"So that was my first day, there were tears, there was anger, there was everything and it really opened me up for the rest of the schedule so much so that there was no stopping me after that!"

We talk some more and her excitement grows with each breath. During her travels she has had a beginning, a becoming and now a personal dawn. I ask if she can see her destination and what it is she wants to achieve.
"My goal is to be the best at my craft and master the profession I have chosen, and I'm willing to work my ass off to get there. I want to achieve the dreams I have and reach the materialistic goals I have set for myself because for me that's an achievement and that's it I guess, then one day to settle down and have kids."

This spurs off us joking about what her kids will be like given her ultra cool image and youthful lingo, imagining them to be born in denims, donning shades and pointing to get people's attention with a Yo!. By now I think the maid must think we've gone mad, but it's ok, it's just the wonderfully mad world of Amrita Arora.

The topic shifts to London as she keenly absorbs my rantings about the Queen, Blair and British weather, latching onto my every word, and before I know it I'm sitting amidst an avid lover of London, who enthusiastically lets me know what she thinks of the place I'm starting to miss.

"I LOVE LONDON!" she exclaims with glee. "I love everything about that place! The buzz, the shopping, the weather – I know people hate the weather but I love it, the monarchy and London is just so classy, it spells class and spells life. I know people are in awe of America and it's larger than life, but it's also very intimidating. For me, London has it all and it has SO many Asians there that you feel like you're at home away from home. The Indians there have kept their culture and their values and they're living the same life as here except in a much more beautiful place."

She knows her stuff and talks from experience, having been a prominent person backstage at the Millennium Masti show two years back. I marvel at how much she knows of my hometown despite never having lived there for a long period of time, and I pick up that this is another of her many skills: to make the most of all she does and gain the maximum from every experience. As a common friend calls to announce her arrival, we decide to wrap up

and ask her to say something to the people reading. She looks down for a second, smiles and then slowly raises here eyes to meet mine. With the same positive vibe and bubbliness she says:
"Go and watch my film, a lot of hard work has gone into it and please appreciate it for what it is, try to look at it as objectively as possible and enjoy it!"

As we wait for her guest to arrive, we go on talking and discuss the film industry, the future and lots more, making me realise that there's so much more to this young angel than meets the eye. Her infectious chirpiness and simple smile have a charming quality that immediately draws your attention to her, and then her personality just steals your heart. The girl who I first met a few nights ago and thought was rather short is destined for big things…because good things happen to good people, and where Amrita is concerned, I'm certain she'll be ranked among the best. Keep watching the sky, a bright star is about to shine.

Fuad Omar

ARJUN RAMPAL: SOARING HIGH

Mumbai. Film City's Helipad location for the shooting of the forthcoming Vipul Shah movie Aankhen, in India's sweltering December heat. As I climb to the top of the mini mountain I wonder why anyone would want to get closer to the sun and shoot so high until I reach the peak and see the view. It's a fitting location for the man I am about to meet, because his ascent too has been swift and one that has reached a height unfathomable for a newcomer in such a short time. But as you're about to learn, Arjun Rampal, the heartthrob actor who's causing hysteria back in London, has no idea of the scale of his success.

When I meet Arjun he's about to give a shot with Akshay Kumar, and after the introductions, he tells me to chill and relax in his room where it's cooler and he'll be with me in a minute. Sporting what looks like a tight fitting M&S black top, he enters his room disgruntled to find the AC isn't working and so promptly shifts us to another room. As the day goes by we get chatting. I tell him about the UK's response to his movies, he tells me about what he's up to and how I better get used to the heat because it never gets cold in Mumbai. He's called for another shot, then it's time for a lunch break. Against my own judgement I give in to his requests and eat lunch, although I have reservations after suffering from food poisoning the day before (not from his food may I add). After eating he has another shot when I fall asleep only to be woken by his baritone voice booming "Arrey mera dost so gaya!" as he walks in smiling. Sensing he can't leave me alone for a few minutes without me catching forty winks, he invites me onto the sets to watch the last shot before a brief break. After that, back in the now-cooler and AC-adjusted room, we begin our interview.

"When I was a little boy my mind kept changing as to what I wanted to be, according to the needs of my family," he tells me with those deep dark eyes fixed on my sleepy beady ones.
"When we didn't have a car I wanted to be a taxi driver, and when my father used to smoke cigarettes I wanted to be a paanwallah so I could sell cigarettes to him! But I think most of all I wanted to be very sporty and excel in sports because that's what I really loved. I loved watching athletics and doing athletics too like the 400 metres race; I excelled in that but then gave it up, but that was one thing I would really have liked to do."

Arjun sits relaxed in his chair, paying careful attention to my every question yet answering everything I throw his way casually and given he's just fed me a delicious lunch it's pretty hard for me not to settle into a laidback mood too. Arjun may be a new face for many of us, but at home in India he's already a known celebrity from his high profile modelling resume. I ask how the boy who wanted to be in athletics ventured into modelling and again the reassuring smile returns.

"It just happened man!" he says rocking back slightly in his chair with a laugh.
"I was at the stage where I had just finished school and was about to join college, and I was at a nightclub called RJ's in Bombay, which was quite a happening nightclub at that

time. Mr Rohit Bal saw me there and he asked me if I was interested in modelling. I didn't know him because I was not into modelling and was not into fashion either so I thought he was just pulling my leg. Then he gave me his card and said 'Give me a call if you're interested'. I went to Delhi for college and while there went to another nightclub called Ghungroo and I met him there, because he's from Delhi and he recognised me. I thought this guy was serious and he said 'It'd be good pocket money so why don't you just try it? I'm sure you'll be good at it.' So I thought ok and gave it a shot. One afternoon I started my bike, went to this shoot and in this hot, sweltering heat we shot with a photographer whose first shoot it was too, and the next day when I saw the pictures I was completely blown! I was like 'This is the way I look? What is this!' I mean the only photograph I had seen of mine was one taken on those normal cameras and at that time even those were pretty bad, so I really thought this was really good, and he said you can do it, so it sort of turned out that the photographer Rohit was a family friend and we became close and I started modelling. So I owe it to him in a way that I got into this field and it started from there, suddenly I realised there's a complete profession in it, I moved to Bombay and things just changed, my life just…changed."

He tells the story of a simple twist of fate that changed his life as though it still comes as a surprise to him. He laughs in between in disbelief at how things have happened and smiles as though he's telling someone else's story of how fortune has favoured a good friend of his, such is the humility of Arjun Rampal, the new kid on the block who has sent waves rippling across international waters in the space of a few months. It's not that hard to believe why he doesn't quite sound assured when I tell him how well he's doing overseas, since he is such a down-to-earth guy. He's genuinely happy at the public enthusiasm to his work and the acceptance by the international audience and when I tell him about the incident at a certain cinema in London where a small crowd of onlookers formed to gaze at his picture on a Pyaar Ishq aur Mohabbat poster, his eyes widen with joy, "What are you saying man!" exclaims telling me this is stuff I should be telling his producers, which neatly leads me to asking how the good looking boy-turned model came across the world of films.

"I was shooting a commercial with Shekhar Kapur and Ashok Mehta was the cameraman for that, that's when I met him for the first time," he says again making certain he acknowledges all the milestones who have helped further his career.

"We spent ten days together and then he said 'I've got this script and I think you should read it'. I said I have no idea about acting and he said 'Everybody acts, I'll make you act, don't worry about that' and I still said that I didn't want to do it and that I'm really not into it. Plus I was going abroad to model in London and New York for a year so he said 'It'll take me about that much time to set it up, so just think about it deeply and let me know'. I thought about it a lot and read the script and really liked it and while I was in New York modelling I made a lot of friends from NYU Film School who were studying Filmmaking, and I was quite intrigued too about going behind the camera at that point and I wanted to study it. When I came back to Bombay after a year and was going to back to the States to study filmmaking and model at the same time, Ashokji was still there with the same confidence and perseverance that I just said let's try it. I thought I'd do six months of modelling and do six months there and six months here and see how it goes. When I got into it I was hooked from day one…up until now."

His eyes narrow as he smiles again, with a look that suggests he has for now found what he's been searching for. He was unaware of modelling and his good looks but after the cajoling of others gave it a shot, the same with films and now he's smugly living and breathing films. Spot him on the sets of Aankhen where he plays a blind man and see how with joyous enthusiasm he shows off his Braille watch that helps the blind man tell time. Even if he's giving a shot wearing dark glasses he won't look at who he's talking to just as a blind man can't and he loves doing what he's doing right now, (which is probably a good thing considering a lot of people seem to too).

"Also when I got into acting I realised I can't do both professions at the same time so I gave up modelling completely, so I wasn't making any money or being distracted by any other work, I only wanted to concentrate on this film (Moksh) and get it right. It took a lot of time but nobody anticipated that and it was ok because throughout I was learning a lot. It was a transitional time where the more I learnt the more comfortable I got in front of the camera as an actor. I saw good results and that just kept me going, and then Rajiv Rai happened," he says once more, matter-of-factly.

"I knew him from before as I had done a music video with him and he told me 'You're versatile and you should get into acting' and I said no way and again he too said 'let's see' and then he went abroad, came back saw some of my rushes from Moksh and Jadh and got really excited. That's literally how Pyaar Ishq aur Mohabbat happened which completely changed the Indian film industry and audiences everywhere suddenly realised this is the guy who's coming into films, which is something that never happened with Moksh because it was a very underplayed thing. Rajiv's film had a big banner, a big director and people woke up to it and offers started really pouring in."

I ask if the filmi press who have cultivated a Casanova image of the new heartthrob (which I can say is not true) have ever got to him, given he's only been in the industry a short while and hasn't escaped the jaws of gossip columnists and critics alike. He exhales a breath of dismissal and shakes his head a little saying:

"See, my philosophy is very simple. I want to make films to entertain audiences and make them feel happy and if they're happy I'm happy (smiles). So if a film critic doesn't like you, that's too bad for him, because I'd rather make five million people happy than try to make just five people happy or five magazines happy. A lot of times people misquote, misinterpret things and write gossip which I guess sells their magazines in today's world, which is sad. If that's the way someone makes their livelihood then good for them, but it doesn't affect me at all because I know who I am. I work hard at what I do which is entertain people to put a smile on their face, make a tear roll down their eyes and that's what's important to me, that's my creativity and the job I do. I'm only concerned with that and don't bother about all these other things."

In the span of three films Arjun has played a romantic hero, a lover scorned and an action man, so already he is working against the grain of typecasting. He agrees this is a conscious move as he doesn't want an expectation to arise from his name about the genre of the movie such that people associate him only as an action hero or a romantic one. Given the scenes I've witnessed on the sets today, his comedic timing is certainly something that's taken me by surprise. So he explains why with him you can never tell what to expect.

"I don't want to create an image where I'm known for doing action or comedy or just romantic roles. I think I'd like to surprise the audience each time and as I grow as an actor I want to go beyond their expectations of me and surpass it so by the next film they expect more from me, that's my challenge."

Given this is his first full fledged UK interview, I ask him what he thinks of London and he smiles once more.
"I've lived in London and modelled there while I was working and I had a great time there. I was staying at Notting Hill Gate and it was great fun, some good experience and some great Chinese food," he says laughing.

A knock on the door informs him he is needed elsewhere and he says he's doing an interview to buy us some more time, so I wrap things up with the new hunk who's wooing the world by asking him to give a message directly to his fans. He thinks for a second then holds the dictafone close and says:

"I promise my fans that every film I'll do is one that I believe in and is done with sincerity, nobody wants to make bad films, sometimes you get it right sometimes you don't but I'll always try to never disappoint them. Whatever work I do it's because I believe in it."

Knowing I have a little more time I can't resist asking what is fast becoming my trademark question and an inside joke among some circles. I ask which ability he would most like to possess: the ability to fly, be invisible or go back in time. "Wow," is his response, before he answers with a smile. Thinking out loud he talks me through his logic and eliminates them one by one saying:
"I wouldn't like to be invisible because then I'd find out things I wasn't meant to. I wouldn't want to go back in time because I prefer to live in the present, and so I guess that leaves just one option: I'd like to fly. I'd like to see what it's like to be a bird, high in the sky, it's something everyone wants to do, if I could fly for a day I'd fly."

Little does he know he already is. Arjun Rampal has been launched into the sky and he's already being looked up to by many with eyes full of wonder and amazement. He's achieving a star status and becoming more and more out of reach as each day goes by because he's flying so high and he doesn't even know it. That's why Arjun will continue to succeed, because whatever magic is in him, he doesn't even realise he has it…all he knows…is he wants to touch his fans' hearts and make them smile.

Fuad Omar

I got into this field and it started from there. Suddenly I realised there's a complete profession in it. I moved to Bombay and things just changed, my life just...changed."

He tells the story of a simple twist of fate that changed his life as though it still comes as a surprise to him. He laughs in between in disbelief at how things have happened and smiles as though he's telling someone else's story of how fortune has favoured a good friend of his, such is the humility of Arjun Rampal.

He's genuinely happy at the public enthusiasm to his work and the acceptance by the international audience and when I tell him about the incident at a certain cinema in London where a small crowd of onlookers formed to gaze at his picture on a Pyaar Ishq aur Mohabbat poster, his eyes widen with joy 'What are you saying man?' he exclaims pointing out that this is stuff I should be telling his producers, which neatly feeds me to asking how the good looking boy turned model came across the world of films.

Milestone

"I was shooting a commercial with Shekhar Kapur and Ashok Mehra was the cameraman for that, that's when I met him for the first time." He says again making certain he acknowledges all the milestones who have helped further his career.

"We spent ten days together and then he said 'I've got this script and I think you should read it.'

"I said I have no idea about acting and he said 'Everybody acts, I'll make you act, don't worry about that' and I still said that I didn't want to do it and that I'm really not into it. Plus I was going abroad to model in London and New York for a year so he said 'It'll take me about that much time to get it up, so just think about it deeply and let me know'.

"I thought about it a lot and read the script and really liked it and while I was in New York modelling I made a lot of friends from NYU Film School who were studying Film making, and I was quite intrigued too about going behind the camera and I wanted to study it. When I came back to Bombay after a year and was going to back to the States to study film making and model at the same time. Anyway was still there with the same confidence and perseverance – so I just said let's try it.

"I thought I'd do six months of modelling and do six months there and six months here and see how it goes. When I got into it I was hooked from day one... up until now.'

Spot him on the sets of Aankhen where he plays a blind man and see how with joyous enthusiasm he shows off his Braille watch that helps the blind men tell time. Even if he's giving a shot wearing dark glasses he won't look at who he's talking to just as a blind man can't and he loved doing what he's doing right now, (which is probably a good thing considering a lot of people seem to) look.

"Also when I got into acting I realised I can't do both professions at the same time so I gave up modelling completely, which meant I wasn't making any money or being distracted by any other work. I only wanted to concentrate on this film (Moksh) and get it right. It took a lot of time but nobody anticipated that and it was ok because throughout I was learning a lot. It was a transitional time where the more I learned the more comfortable I got in front of the camera as an actor. I saw good results and that just kept me going and then Rajiv Rai happened," he says with more matter-of-factly.

"I knew him from before as I had done a music video with him and he told me 'You're versatile and you should get into acting' and I said no way and again he insisted and 'let's see' and then he went ahead came back say some of my scenes from Moksh and Jmeh and got really excited.

"That's literally how Pyaar Ishq aur Mohabbat happened which completely changed the Indian film industry and audiences everywhere suddenly realised this is a guy who's carrying two films, which is something that never happened with Moksh, because it was a very underplayed thing."

"Rajiv's film had a big banner, a big director and people woke up to it and offers started really pouring in."

I ask if the film press who have cultivated a Casanova image of the new heartthrob (which I can say is not true) have ever got to him, given he's only been in the industry a short while and hasn't escaped the jaws of gossip columnists and critics alike. He exhales a breath of demand and shakes his head a little saying:

Gossip

"See, my philosophy is very simple. I want to make films to entertain audiences and make them feel happy and if they're happy I'm happy period.

"So if a film critic doesn't like you, that's too bad for him, because I'd rather make five million people happy than try to make five magazines happy.

"A lot of times people misquote, misinterpret things and write gossip which I guess sells their magazines in today's world, which is sad if that's the way someone makes their livelihood then good for them, but it doesn't affect me at all because I know who I am.

"I work hard... people to put... and roll down... important to me... job I do. I'm on... don't bother ab...

Given this is... interview, I ask... and he smiles...

"I've lived in... while I was wor... there, I was sta... was great fun... some of the be..." he says laughin...

A knock on the... needed elsewher... interview to buy... things up with... the world by ac... directly to his fa... then holds the g...

"I promise my... one film I belie... sincerity, nob... sometimes you... don't bet I'll als... disappoint them... because I believe...

Many believe... him worldwide... He's achieving a... flying so high a... That's why Arju...

Fuad Omar

> "If a film critic doesn't like me, that's too bad for him, because I'd rather make five million people happy than try to make five magazines happy."

RAVEENA TANDON: INSTANT NIRVANA

As I head up 14 floors to Raveena's apartment, a million questions run through my head. I have met her numerous times before while covering her events but never actually interviewed her. Given her huge status I am tempted to ask a barrage of questions which would exhaust her entry into films, her struggle and more recently her performances in films with a social message. But as it is my first with her I'm also attracted into asking her questions following a biblical fashion with three different in-depth interviews such as Genesis, the struggle and Revelation. The lift stops and my time to think is up.

A simple white marbled apartment greets me with friendly surroundings and her father welcomes me warmly. The rush begins now as Raveena pops out from her office and says "Sorry, just five minutes, I'm just wrapping up a narration" before disappearing back into the room. She has a very unapproachable picture painted by wild accusations and the nay-sayers have polished up on ammunition regarding her reputation, yet my first impression is of the smile with which she greeted me two years ago and her friendly demeanour ever since and the now concerned Raveena who came out of her office to personally apologise for the delay. For all those who are expecting starry hang ups: Prepare for disappointment.

Seated in her cosy office I begin the interview by reminding her how since the beginning of her career she has been coming back by popular demand every year to London for stage shows.

"Luckily I've been doing shows since the beginning of my career, in fact I think I must be the heroine with the maximum number of world tours. I came in 1992, 1994, 1995 then 1998, this year with the Millennium Masti and I'm coming again in March-April next year."

It must be an ecstatic feeling to be loved so much abroad that you are constantly called back, I wonder aloud asking how she feels about all this affection and warmth from the desis who are abroad.

"I think it's great, overseas I've had a great market because the fact that I'm called again and again, I don't think any other heroine has gone so many times. It's a great feeling, especially being there on stage and the fans are all screaming for you, it's a different high altogether. I do it for that instant thrill, it's like instant nirvana. You just reach this totally new level of high that nothing can beat it, it's just the best."

I ask if she recalls her debut stage show and what it felt like to be on stage for the first time and she smiles again, telling me:

"I remember it was 1992, the show was titled Chamakte Sitare. It had me, Aamir, Salman, Divya Bharti and Juhi Chawla. When I first came on I was really nervous, I thought I'd black out. I think that never goes, even today still I feel that sense of panic and level of excitement and you're all pepped up thinking I hope nothing goes wrong. And it's like when you suddenly take that first step onto the stage from the wings and up until that point there are butterflies, but the second you hear the screams it's all over. Then all of a sudden you're there in front of thousands of people, giving them your best because they are there and have all turned up to appreciate you. Those cheers are priceless and you just feel great about the whole thing, it's indescribable."

If it can assured that Raveena always gives her best at her stage shows, it can also be guaranteed that her fans do not come unprepared, with boards and hoardings expressing undying love for her or placards of support, the signs and gifts brought to the auditoriums in hope that she may notice someone has gone to such trouble for her are always present. I wonder if she has ever noticed these efforts while on stage, and if that direct interaction is really there. She smiles and cannot hold back a grin the size of Mumbai itself, and answers:
"Yes, yes, of course, we do see all those wonderful things. We see the teddy bears and all, it's unbelievable. "

She pauses as her eyes twinkle as though she is being reminded of that stage magic and turns to me to sum up how important stage shows are to her and how much she loves the support fans clearly turn out in their droves to give.
"Believe me, it's even more fun and even more rewarding than doing a good film. Because if you've done a good film and its released somewhere in some theatre, you don't know or get to see who's cheering for you or clapping, you have no live interaction with the audience. Someone could be clapping for you 5000 miles away and you won't hear it,

but on stage I hear every clap. It's live and the response is right there in front of you. It's simply incredible."

On that note I am served possibly what could be the best tea I have ever had, and for seconds after my first sip I am transported to my own nirvana of heavenly bliss. Temptation beckons for me to just sit back and relax to enjoy this extremely well made tea but on being brought back to her cosy home, I realise in the company of a friend I hardly notice that I am working.

I ask about how she has managed to make sure that she graces every magazine cover month after month, even when her films aren't doing well, she agrees the exposure is there, but is honest in her reaction that she cannot take the credit for any PR work.

"I guess I can sum it up by saying I think I'm plain and simply lucky. As far as PR work is concerned there is none. I don't even have a PR officer working for me. In fact you know what, someone called me up yesterday and said 'look you're on the cover of the latest G magazine', and I got a copy and was surprised. You see, half the time I don't even know I'm on the cover until the magazine comes out. But I don't have a PR and I'm not into calling people and saying put me on the cover of a magazine and it actually comes as a surprise to me when I'm told I'm on this magazine or that cover."

I take another sip of the finely brewed tea and nod my head as I settle more and more into a comfort zone in the air conditioned, homely surroundings.

"Fortunately I can say I've been lucky because after Pathar ke Phool I had quite a few duds, but thankfully even though I was going through that sort of phase I kept signing good films with good directors. They never lost confidence in me or faith in my talent or whatever you want to call it, so I kept going on. Then suddenly came these five-six superhits in a row like Andaaz Apna Apna, Laadla, Imtihan, Dilwale, Mohra, Khiladiyon ka Khiladi. That's when I thought okay, things are going well you know, as it was it was never my ambition to become an actress and this has never been for me the be all and end all. It's been a rollercoaster ride, there have been ups and downs but that's what life's all about. Where there's a will there's a way."

I remind Raveena how I've been following her career since I became interested in Hindi films and how I was glad to see a growth in her performances from Patthar ke Phool to Kshatriya to date in that the improvement can always be seen and never faulted by critics. She nods her head agreeingly, thankful I've noticed and contemplates:

"You see, that's another thing I've been lucky about. Sometimes even though my films didn't do well the media always spotted a good performance and said she has performed well or wrote good about me. Maybe it helped in encouraging me to hang on. You see after Mohra the way it was I gave up working for about two years. In those two years everyone who started out with me like Karisma and Manisha all evolved as actresses with Raja Hindustani and Bombay. During the time I was to evolve from being a glamour doll to a more serious actress, I sat back and gave up work, so when I came back I had to catch up and reach that stage. The evolution could have been done in less time but it's because I took a break in between which slowed the whole process down."

The growth of Raveena is also clearly evident in the more recent ventures she has participated in, such as E.Niwas' Shool and the forthcoming Kalpana Lajmi movie, both which presented Raveena in a different light and were films with a social message.

"I have two films about to release Daman and Aks, where the roles are in total contrast. In Aks I play a club dancer and it's a glamorous role and Daman is very, very different. Then I'm also doing a bilingual project with Kamal Hassan called Abhay, then there's Anees Bazmi's Deewangi with Sanjay and Ajay, Akhiyan se Goli Maare with Govinda and Ek Hindustani with Sunil Shetty and a few others."

The topic moves on to fans and fanmail. We know that she has such strong public support and receives fanmail. Does she get time to read her fanmail, does she ever reply, I ask.

"I love to read my fanmail and sometimes whenever I have time I reply to the really nice ones as well. But you get all sorts of mail, sometimes you get scary ones as well bordering on obsession. There was one man who wrote to me who believed we were married and he wrote to me saying when will you come back home to me and the kids, the kids are crying! The neighbours can't handle the kids anymore and all this, you get wacko ones as well but mostly it's all good feedback. Some of the most touching and best letters I've received are from the girls who have read my interviews and said I am very philosophical and some see you as an inspiration which is so nice. There are some who write and say we went through a tough time but after reading your interviews that even stars go through these problems and it helps pull us through, so I love letters like that which give me the feeling that when I talk it does make a difference to people."

"My father always said when a child learns to walk he falls a hundred times, but you have to keep getting up or you'll never learn to walk. My parents are my role models, they've been the best teachers I've ever had. I wish that when I have kids I can raise them as well as they have raised me."

The phone rings and she is informed her next appointment awaits her, so I eye the time and ask her to wind up with a message to her fans and everyone reading all around the world.

"Every individual human being can make a difference, be it a good deed a day or something as small as a smile, it can go a long way and make a difference. I'd like to say to my well wishers as that's what they are more than my fans because they've given me so much strength, that one small step can make a difference. One little contribution works a long way. I believe in humanity being the biggest religion of all, and unfortunately I think humankind's worst enemy is human beings themself, with all this fighting and bad things happening, where's it's all going to lead? You don't take any bad things with you when you go, only the good things, so make the difference."

On that note she nods her head with a smile, as if to tell herself there is still hope for the world if everyone tries, and as I finish off my tea she bursts with energy and takes my dictaphone playfully, speaking directly to all reading and says, "Yes people, spread the good word!".

Fuad Omar

INTRODUCING VIVEK OBEROI

I went to meet Vivek Oberoi and didn't get my interview. It's not that he kept me waiting, was too busy or simply has stopped talking to the press, but read on and you'll find out why there's no interview. However my meeting with Vivek Oberoi was one where I probably got more out of him than if I had interviewed him.

I first met Vivek on the sets of Dum, when I popped in to see a friend. A jeweller's shop had been transformed into a film set packed with lights, hoards of people outside trying to catch glimpses of what was going on inside every time the door opened and was my first glimpse of the much touted newcomer. I was leaving for London and had dropped by to say farewell to a dear friend when she said, "You must meet this young man, he's going to be the next big thing…". Those are literally the words that echo in my mind every time I recount our first meeting. She walked over and introduced me to a tall, tanned man who had a charming smile, a firm handshake and was full of conversation that exuded warmth and honesty. We connected instantly. Five minutes later and we were talking about London, New York and becoming friends, leaving the person who I came to see calling me every five minutes.

That was when I first met Vivek Oberoi. This time, armed with my Dictaphone, questions that probed the mind and attempted to explain exactly his stand in Indian cinema at this precise moment of time, I journeyed off to Walkeshwar, which for those who don't know Mumbai is in town. When I see him on the sets of a forthcoming film, the first thing I notice is that he seems to have lost weight since I last saw him and his smile is just as reassuring. He greets me and allows me to escape from the Mumbai heat, ensuring I'm well looked after with refreshments, a sofa and an air conditioner blowing in my face. Minutes later he emerges and we strike up a conversation so quickly it's like landing on your feet running. We spend a few minutes catching up on what's been happening since we last met in our respective lives and sporting a glimpse of tiredness in his eyes, I ask about how work is. He smiles and says it's good before going on to explain he's just worked straight through the last 34 hours and has no intention of stopping soon. He's tired and being worked like a machine, yet his enthusiasm is on overdrive. Like a child who doesn't want to close his eyes in case he misses something, Vivek is working round the clock to the best of his ability and succeeding in creating magic on celluloid. Few have seen him on screen when I write this, but the rushes I've seen of some of his debut venture Company's scenes and what I've seen of Dum in the on-set monitor is enough to arouse interest.

"I've conditioned myself to nap, which is something I could never do before," he tells me, smiling. "I catch a few hours of sleep here and there and it works."

After realising our common passion for cinema, its nuances, details and the attention paid to creating a moment on celluloid that will be documented forever, we are caught up in a verbal sparring session feeding off each other and moving from topic to topic at speeds that cut like a razor. If there's one open door I cannot resist, it's discussing my favourite medium, industry and profession and I take the bait. I make a comment on the pain some actors go through for their roles and the passion with which they happily leap from tall buildings and break their knees dancing because they love their art so much and realise that while pain is momentary, film is forever. Vivek tells me about his action sequences and how scared he was when giving his first action take which he had to do again for continuity's sake immediately after he experienced the satisfying rush that follows completing something you've set out to do with a bout of adrenalin. Vivek has full faith in his action directors and through leaving the responsibility with them has performed more action in the past few months than I've done in a lifetime.

Vivek is tall, good looking and oozes charisma. His confidence is to his advantage because when he tells you something can be done, no matter how impossible, you believe it can be. He's not taking the conventional clean-shaven hero riding-on-a-motorbike-with-a-girl-on-his-arm route with his debut film, which shows him on the hoarding at Juhu sporting a beard and moustache, a cigarette tightly meshed between his teeth and a menacing look that commands attention. He's exciting and grabs your attention in every frame you see him, but is already experiencing media hype pre his film's release. He's been called in the past few days "the best thing to happen to Bollywood", "the next Hrithik Roshan" and a "legend in the making" but the praise does not daunt him nor does he succumb to the game the media is trying to play with him. "My film hasn't even released yet and they're saying these things," he says shaking his head. I tell him about the oft-too-familiar path those before him have had to take which involves the media building you up for months and then as soon as you displease them they bring you crashing down beginning an in-print tirade aimed at crucifying your career. My words are repeated back to me as Vivek knows and has seen this all before. He's not about to fall into any trap because he knows his medium and knows his job. Success to him is successfully portraying the character he's agreed to adopt and convincingly contributing towards good cinema, and through what he says he's most excited because he's being allowed to give his all to everything he's doing. In what totally blows me away for the next ten minutes, Vivek takes me on a visual and empathic trip through the characters he's portraying in the next few months. Starting with Chandu from Company he mouths some dialogues to me threateningly and his mannerisms change instantly giving me a Primal Fear Edward Norton complex. He tells me how he spent time in slums observing the way people walked, sat, talked and behaved and mimicked them to the hilt, as though this was his education. His dedication led him to make himself look seven shades darker than his natural skin colour to successfully assay the role. Next up he is his character from Dum and gets up to show me how this man walks, whose psyche is of a victim of circumstance. Before I know it I've seen seven shades to Vivek myself and have felt each character as if I know them myself, that's how convincingly he runs through each one. And it's not just mannerisms he's created but also each one speaks differently, one with a slang, the other in a soft-spoken delicate tone, and when he starts talking normally I'm slightly disoriented for a while as I get my feet back to reality and the real Vivek Oberoi.

The creativity, spontaneity and immense dedication to studying and living each role he takes on is Vivek's trump card and he's not even playing poker. He's not in the game to win, but to be true to his art. He's here to do good work and give good performances and given his knowledge of cinema, he has every potential within him to conquer his medium and achieve the satisfaction he craves. I am not going to say Vivek Oberoi is a legend in the making nor state without seeing his film he's an ace artiste, but what I will say is he's definitely an actor that excites me. He has in him a crackling flame that burns brighter with every new thing he learns, and will slowly become an engulfing inferno that has the potential to set Indian cinema on fire and push forward our industry in terms of performance and professionalism.

I came to meet Vivek and didn't get my interview because we ended up passively discussing cinema and delving in conversations that mirrored our common goals and love for the medium. I went to meet Vivek Oberoi and didn't get my interview…but I got so much more: A rare glimpse into the mind of the actor who is as excited about his roles as those who are writing them and a man who knows so much about and understands cinema like few people do, and what's most exciting is that he's still growing.
"Change will always happen, but growth is what matters," is something he said to me that rings through my ears as I leave the building.

Vivek Oberoi is someone who is one to watch, because as long as he keeps asking questions he'll always be the answer. Plus he owes me an interview.

Fuad Omar

MADHURI DIXIT: THE JOURNEY

Madhuri Dixit is undoubtedly the Queen of Indian cinema. Her career spans a string of successful films and her performances are legendary, be they on the big screen or on stage. Her latest release Yeh Raaste Pyaar Ke, despite carrying not too promising reports, is packing cinemas everywhere (especially in the UK) and has even done better in its opening week than the other big movie Dil Chahta Hai. The reports of the movie are average but people unanimously agree on the finer point being Madhuri and her performance, as always.

Her next release is Rajkumar Santoshi's Lajja which too is carrying high expectations. The audience just cannot get enough of Madhuri and the 'Madhuri Magic' continues with her every release.

Her startling quantum leap from anonymity to ubiquity is one that has dispelled many calculations of Bollywood pundits and left many astrologers impoverished. Her lightning success story after a struggle of 6 years is an example of one of today's stars who has influenced the life of many an Indian and is heralded by some as an ambassador of the country.

In 1984 the shy teenager made her debut in a Rajshri film *Abodh* which was soon forgotten, leaving the heroine to the same fate. Ten years later a confident 'number one' actress stars in the biggest hit of the century, Rajshri's *Hum Aapke Hain Koun..!* and the superstars megastar status is reaffirmed.

Critics argued that the film was too sweet and she left some with a diabetic syndrome, but the fact was she mesmerised on screen and everyone's eyes were fixed on her throughout, following her unknowingly. Since her dramatic entry on roller-skates in the film, and as she sang and waltzed through the picture, handling professionally the most complicated and emotionally demanding role effortlessly, she had the entire audience enthralled and India captive to 'Madhuri Mania'. With her perfect lip-synching, an impeccable Urdu pronunciation (despite being of Maharashtrian origin) and her command of a galaxy of expressions as well as being pleasing to the eye, a shining star had seemingly been born out of a dwindling meteor. But then, given her enviable reservoir of talent, this was inevitable and she personifies the ultimate female Indian star.

Madhuri's presence in the peacock screen is one which holds high expectation and increases the distribution price of a film, along with its credibility and box office draw. In the industry famous for being fraught with routine back stabbings, petty politics, jealousy, cut-throat competition and largely blind superstition, her struggle and success proves she is a survivor and winner of the public's affection and prayers. Her transition from a passive zombie, only good for coy smiles and heaving or bursting into kathak or dico, to a self assertive, visible entity is unmistakable. The Hindi film heroine today has plum roles thanks to Madhuri's power and stance in the industry. The past 17 years have been years of learning she modestly confesses, but also the ones that transformed her into every newcomer's inspiration, every new hero's dream and new heroine's idol.

Her success was initially credited to her hit pairing with veteran actor Anil Kapoor, but this myth was fast disproved when two consecutive films starring the favourites, *Jeevan Ek Sangharsh* and *Jamai Raja*, flopped miserably. Similarly when her dancing skills and good numbers were deemed responsible for her success she gave a flop with *Sailaab*, a dancing extravaganza, establishing herself as a talent whose success factor could not be pin pointed to one or two attributes. Her first film *Abodh* in 1984, was a flop, as were her five subsequent films, but she hit back in 1989 as she became known as the "Ek-Do-Teen" girl for *Tezaab*, which gave her dancing and acting scope to prove she had some fire in her. She strengthened her position in 1990 with *Ram Lakhan* and has not looked back since. Although her laser eyed histrionics in *Tezaab* won her rapturous reviews and she gave a comic resonance to the 1990 film *Dil*, the spotlight was only about to shine brightest on the rising superstar.

Today she is regarded as a self made celebrity and superstar and clearly the most versatile actress in Bollywood. Her film alone carries a film and makes it a must-see and her star power demands roles be written especially with her in mind. While some claim her dazzling smile leaves hearts fluttering and her charismatic roles are haunting, others say there is no explanation for the Madhuri Magic. No specific factors make Madhuri who she is, but one major plus point is her Indian-ness. While studying media, I read a book on stars and found a reference which seemed to spell out Madhuri to the core: Richard Dyers work in his book *Stars* categorically states stars exist because of a reservoir of talent, which according to him include "striking photogenic looks, acting ability, presence on camera, charm and personality, sex appeal, attractive voice and bearing", which to any Indian reads like a checklist of Madhuri's strengths.

The superhit film *Saajan* put Madhuri firmly on the map and left many expectations for her to live up to. In 1992 she earned a sex symbol status as she made India's male population's hearts go "dhak dhak" and stunned with a convincing performance in *Beta* for which she gained a Filmfare Award for Best Actress. Her next release *Sangeet* did not fare well and this began a bad year, but it was soon made clear flops no longer affected Madhuri's star status as she was loved by the public in her every appearance and it seemed the press were the ones eager to pull her down with every silver screen failure. But 1993 saw the release of the eagerly awaited Subhash Ghai film and Sanjay Dutt- Jackie Shroff- Madhuri Dixit starrer *Khalnayak* again in which her presence was prominent. The film was shrouded with controversy as the film's hero-cum-villain Sanjay Dutt was arrested in an arms possession case and the song "Choli ke Peechay Kya Hai" caused great pre-release tension. However the song may have tweaked conservative sensibilities, but with the aid of choreographer Saroj Khan's magnetic movements and Madhuri's innocence, the song and dance number became a kind of mass market art form, and the film was passed by censors with few cuts. The Indian audience made it 1993's biggest hit and Madhuri was loved by all as she became heralded as the new numero uno actress by the media in their fickle numbers game which they constantly attach to cinema's stars.

After this rumours of a contemporary actress Juhi Chawla overtaking her in the battle for the number one slot were ripe as Juhi was present in the hits, and Madhuri's films were not making the expected impact. The press were quick to respond, touting Juhi as their new favourite and Madhuri maintained a dignified stance refusing to be sucked into such controversies and comment, enlightening the press in an interview of the public reaction:

"The numbers game is media made. They try and place you on a pedestal or write you off with every release. The audiences are less fickle and narrow-minded, they are in the cinemas purely for entertainment. I am touched by the fiercely loyal fans I have who write to these magazines whenever they write something not-so-flattering about me. I am not a superstar and am not aware of the impact I have on people's lives. I am just an ordinary girl enjoying my work, and my efforts are being appreciated."

1994 proved the rumours wrong as Juhi gave not a single hit and Madhuri's *Anjaam* with Shahrukh Khan released and flopped, but gained her much critical acclaim for her heart-wrenching and polished performance, considered by some as her finest. The audience began to recognise the characteristic narrowing of her eyes as the indication of an emotional eruption and cheered whenever they sensed this on screen. August 1994 made history as the biggest grossing film of all time was released, Rajshri's *Hum Aapke Hain Koun..!* which ran to packed cinema houses for a period of four years before finally being released on video. Her star status was recognised to the hilt with this movie as she was given top billing over even the film's superstar hero Salman Khan, and more significantly the posters of Sooraj Barjatya's second venture differed greatly from his cult debut film *Maine Pyar Kiya* (1989), showing Madhuri's vitalising woman-of-the-90s image and contribution to Indian cinema. While *Maine Pyar Kiya* showed a docile Bhagyashree at the feet of a bare-chested Salman Khan, *Hum Aapke Hain Koun*'s posters displayed a self possessed Madhuri standing shoulder to shoulder with Salman, confidence writ large on her face. She has evolved from actress to star to superstar to icon. Any misunderstanding of any actress even entering Madhuri's league has been resolved as she wiped out all competition. *Hum Aapke Hain Koun* is not only the biggest film of Madhuri's career, but the biggest grosser of all time, and Madhuri has a lot to do with it.

She picked up a list of awards for her performance including the prestigious Filmfare award and Screen-Videocon Award for Best Actress for the film. She had finally truly established herself and carved a niche as the ultimate female superstar of Indian cinema and is today Bollywood's highest paid heroine, earning a place in the Millennium edition of the Guinness Book of World Records. Hits followed regularly after but every year *Hum Aapke Hain Koun* continued to run like a phenomenon. Madhuri was crowned the queen of Bollywood and her star status reached a level where she was called the 'female Amitabh Bachchan'. Her stage shows sold out and fans flocked to her shootings to catch a glimpse of the ultimate star. She has even been called the peacemaker between India and Pakistan as a Pakistani official joked to a national newspaper on his visit to India, "You can keep Kashmir, just give us Madhuri!"

When I recently met Madhuri on the sets of Sanjay Leela Bhansali's Devdas, she was still the eternal beauty looking better than ever, and I was probably for the first time in years a bundle of nerves. I even remember breaking the ice by telling her, "If I start stammering or fumbling my questions, you'll have to forgive me, it's just that you've given so much to Indian cinema and been the one I watched growing up, so this is a little daunting."

Her response was the trademark Madhuri smile, laced with her gentle laughter as she slowly tilted her head back slightly and responded:
"Oh please! I'm sure you've interviewed much bigger stars than me!".

Ever the modest Madhuri! Meeting Madhuri Dixit is still to this day the highlight of my journalistic and writing career, because she really is a living legend. Judging by the army of fans she has who criticise anyone who dares write against her and the response to her new film, it seems like myself, you too all have her firmly embedded in your hearts as someone who's never need to ask: Hum Aapke Hain Koun?

On the sets of Devdas

JOHN ABRAHAM: SPEED DEMON

It's around 5pm and I'm in West Andheri, Mumbai trying to figure out some directions I've written down on a scrap of paper. I walk outside a shopping mall and take a right only to find myself in what is the smelliest place I've been to. I ask a local for help who laughs saying it seems I'm following my own directions upside down. I go back to the shopping mall and already I'm running late. My mobile rings and the friendly voice says "Fuad! Where are you??". Er, I'm kinda lost I tell the voice and he advises me which direction I should be moving in. It's 5:15 and I was supposed to meet John Abraham, supermodel and soon-to-be-actor at five, and he seems to find my loss of orientation hilarious. He directs me through turns and landmarks on the phone as I relay the message to the rickshaw driver, before the driver himself gets fed up and takes the phone to ask where I want to go. Five minutes later I am outside John Abraham's building and waving goodbye to the irate driver who is glad to see the back of me. I spot Navin Shetty, a friend and associate of Sunil Shetty's and we catch up while walking towards John's place. He meets us half way and sporting a tee shirt, blue denims and a stubble he greets us warmly.

"You finally made it!" he says highlighting my inability to follow directions. After a brief chat with Navin, he grabs me and says "Come on we have to go, I have a really important meeting". He signals to a rickshaw driver and we get in. Realising we're running late and he needs to be somewhere soon and my next meeting is at 6:30 we decide to begin the interview on the way. As we speed down the streets with each corner making me jump half on the road, we begin our conversation.

Those who know who John is will know he's fairer than the average Indian. He informs me of his background and how he's a mixed hybrid that represents the best of both worlds.
"I was born and brought up in Bombay. My father's a South Indian and my mother's Iranian, so I'm a total mixed breed," he says smiling.
The young dude who I now realise I have no idea where he's taking me tells me how modelling happened in between giving directions to the driver.

"I did my MBA specialising in Marketing, and worked with an agency as a media consultant. Some of my school friends who saw I was working out so hard told me 'why don't you get into modelling? Give it a shot, just for the sake of it'. I thought why not and so did a competition called Gladrags in March 1999, and by the grace of God I won!"

At this point the journey takes a Lord of the Rings style acceleration and a pothole in the road means my head goes crashing into the roof of the 3-wheeled wonder and for a minute I'm dazed. John hasn't even noticed and is having the time of his life. His story continues:

"I went for the International Manhunt in the Philippines where the winner of each country competes against each other and so it was pretty big. I came second in the world for that one which was great and that led to things happening. I got signed up with a modelling agency in Singapore and did some modelling there and in Hong Kong and back in India too, which really took off for me. So I decided to pursue modelling here in India in August 1999, and by August 2001 I was shooting for my first movie, so effectively I was a model for just two years."

We enter a quiet side road and the relief on my face shows. I may be asking the questions but no way am I focussed and John too, seems preoccupied in figuring out the best route to wherever we're going. After advising the driver some more, we continue and talk about the second stage of his career which is about to take off: his entry into Bollywood.

"I'm doing a movie with Rahul Rawail whose made great films such as Love Story, Betaab and Arjun Pandit. And it's a good launch pad because he launched Sunny Deol and Kumar Gaurav as well as Aishwarya Rai and Kajol. After that I'm doing a movie with Vikram Bhatt which has Bipasha Basu opposite me and also has Mr Bachchan in it, so I'm extremely fortunate to be working with him at such an early stage of my career. Besides that I have got a lot of international offers but let's see how things work out there."

International waters beckon and John is ready to dive in. He had a blast shooting in Leicester last year and can't wait to return to foreign soil. What does he like most? The fact that no one can figure out where exactly he's from.

"I just went recently to Vancouver and of all the people I spoke to, ninety-nine percent of them thought I was Italian. One said I was Indian, another said Middle Eastern but mostly people thought I was Italian and they liked the mixed look I had. So modelling internationally is something that is high on my agenda and is a priority. It's just a matter of dates and timing, but given the option I'd love to model abroad."

We arrive at our destination wherever it is, and start walking. I ask what he wanted to be when he was younger and his answer reveals why the rickshaw adventure we've just endured was so thrilling for him. He wanted to pretty much be Indiana Jones.

"When I was a kid I wanted to be an archaeologist until around the seventh standard. I was really intrigued by the pyramids and mummies and dinosaurs, I collected lots of books about the wonders of the world and all, but it all changed one day when I decided I wanted to be a soccer player! I captained my school, college and Management Institute and even Bombay in soccer and still follow the sport, especially the English Premier league…I'm a Man U fan!" he says laughing.

We take a turning into what seems like a block of flats but round the back enter an area that seems like a garage. He smiles at the workers and they are glad to see him, requesting before he leaves to allow them to take a photo with him to which he replies, "You guys are the stars, mujhe aapke saath photo keechna chahiye!" We head back towards the front and continue.

"I love English football because it's very fast-paced and you see a lot of goals which is not something you get in other leagues. That's what I wanted to be at that point in time, it was either soccer or biking that I was into. There was also a time I wanted to get into the 500cc championships so I had a lot of things I wanted to do!"

With so many pursuits on the agenda, does he ever get time to make any of them happen?
"Yes of course! Through my films I get the chance to and I also got the chance to meet lots of people and travel a lot and learn so much too. In the US I discovered a school that teaches you so many things like sky diving and more biking so that's something I want to do."
The boys are in a crowd moving towards us, seemingly concealing something between them. John doesn't notice and starts telling me about his forthcoming films.

"Both my movies are action oriented. One's typically a similar film to Betaab, and ..oh man," he says stopping mid-sentence, handing me the Dictaphone. We are at a garage and the workers have wheeled out his new bike which he's just had imported and done up. His reaction to this speed demon is priceless and his eyes light up like a child in a toy store.

"There's my bike..." he says lost in awe, "isn't she beautiful?"

Not being one too familiar with the motorbike scene I comment she looks great and seems to have a lot of power, and he smiles as he straddles his new machine.
"Wanna hear her purr?" he asks as he starts revving up the engine and telling me we have to go for a ride. A few minutes later he's off cloud nine and realises we'd better finish the interview so he can enjoy his bike further. When is he coming back to the UK I ask the man still eyeing the object of his affection.

"I'm in love with the UK and Wales and I'd love to come back there and maybe the future will hold work for me there too."
Since he's in such a passionate mood I ask on the spur of the moment who he'd most like to have lunch with.

"If I could have lunch with anyone it would be Liz Hurley, I think she's gorgeous. Actually she'd be good lunch or dessert! And I love the accent!"

I realise time's pressing on and both our attention is more focussed on his bike than anything else, so I wind up by asking him to briefly mention his movies and give a message.

"Well the first movie is a learning process but the second one's a winner, which I'm very confident about. I've worked very hard and I hope people really like it."

The second he stops the Dictaphone, he's tossed it in my direction and hopped onto his bike. Inviting me for a spin he assures me my decline is my loss and we fix up a time to catch up later. The same rickshaw driver who brought us here agrees to take me to my next destination but not before joining me and the workers in waving goodbye to John Abraham as he dons his shades and speeds off into the sunset. Be prepared, he's heading in your direction…and fast.

Fuad Omar

JACKIE OF ALL TRADES

Jackie Shroff is a man who cannot be kept down. I met him last year when he came first for the International Indian Film Awards, then briefly again when he came for the promotion of Mission Kashmir. The impression I get is that he likes London, and he's always been the same every time I see him, full of warmth and those glazed eyes that say "Hi". The next time we met was on the sets of Bas Itna Sa Khwaab Hai at Mukesh Mills which is in Mumbai for a night shoot which also celebrated his birthday last year, which was wild to say the least.

I speak to Jackie wanting to ask about what his favourite personal memories are, given that firstly he's been in the industry for so long and secondly because he is someone most of today's generation have grown up watching be in Hero, Karma, Kaash or Ram Lakhan, Khalnayak or 1942 A Love Story. I realise how the theme I wish to explore ties in with his last film and so use that to also ask what it is about Yaadein that attracted him to the project, although I could predict his answer given the person he is immediately. What you see in Yaadein is not too different from the Jackie of real life. He's cool, calm and collected and has a loving wife and two adoring children. When watching Yaadein I could almost picture some scenes of Jackie with his daughters being not too different from his real life family as in both he is a doting family man.

I steal a few moments with Jaggu Dada, and ask how the whole media blitzkrieg feels for him given that firstly Yaadein was hyped and secondly that he was given prominent attention given his pivotal role in the movie. Dressed in a black suit and cowboy boots, the suave and sophisticated Shroff looks me in the eye and says:

"I feel very happy bhiddu," he says patting me on the shoulder with a look that says he's relieved this is a relaxed interview and not one full of formal questions or dissections of Yaadein.

I ask him what attracted him to Yaadein and he draws his fingers over his thinly trimmed moustache, before nodding his head and saying:

"I really like Subhash Ghai as a director, as a person and brother, and there's no way I can say no to him, he's been there since the beginning of my career. And the other thing is that the role was very strong and had a unique selling point of being a character that would allow me to show the father daughter relationship. I have three daughters in the film and it deals with how difficult it gets for a father to look after them, to talk with them about their boyfriends and relationships, and how they wouldn't talk to him about these things out of fear that he would dictate to them. But through the film and this role I'm trying to show and encourage that a family should live like friends."

I draw the real life comparison and ask Jackie if as on screen he plays more the friend to his daughter Isha than father, if it is true off screen too with his own two children.

"In real life too, I'm more like a friend to my daughter Krishna and (son) Tiger too, they're like my buddies. They tell me everything that goes on in their life," he says smiling.

"I kept my own daughter as the centre point of inspiration throughout the making of this movie because I know she's going to grow up very fast and I know that she'll have a lot of boyfriends after her! And I want her to be my pal and talk to me about these things, about her feelings and what she goes through. I feel a child should be able to take their parents as their best friends."

Anyone who's seen or met Jackie's children tends to have the incurable illness of never being able to stop talking about them. His son Tiger has the same smile as his father and that deep sensitive look in his eyes, and Krishna is as beautiful as her mum, and eyes that show the purity of her soul, lost in innocence and happy with the world she's in, this she reflects in her ever-bright smile.

We move on and I ask about a story sitting he had a few days back, and he laughs as his eyes widen, saying "Sandhya! How do you know all this! Sangeeth Sivan is the director, Santosh Sivan's younger brother, it'll have Raveena and myself, maybe Chandrachur Singh and one more couple. It's about a killer who goes to kill somebody and how he's hunted, that's all I can say, but it sounds amazing."

I ask him to mention a few of his most memorable films to which he replies "my own films or just any films" and I ask him about his own, based on his experiences in these films.

"Ab khud ka kya pick karoo!" he exclaims before I edge him to give me an answer.
"Bahut saari picture hai… pehli successful picture Hero thi, second successful as an actor was Kaash, when people took notice and said he can act also! And then Parinda that gave me the first award and gave me the chance to work with Vinod Chopra and Nana Patekar. Aar Ya Paar where I

got to play the bad guy for the first time, so these are some of my cherished memories but there are so many good memories and good films I don't want to pick just one. Also I must mention Dev Anand's Guide which is my most favourite film and I can watch that anytime."

Journeying through the Shroff's mind is a trip in itself because his eyes give you the answer before he does. As he remembers old films you can see part of the smile and the reminiscence and seeing him so relaxed makes this feel less like an interview and more like a friendly chat. I move away from the movies and ask his most cherished memory, and he shifts slightly in his seat and looks at me for a second before responding, his eyes glazed deep in thought. Then with a slight smile and thinking back he replies:

"Seeing my little boy in the incubator when he was born and when he was taken into where all the little kids are kept. All the other kids were crying away but he was lying there and he just turned his head and he had a smile on his face. And I just knew this was one kid who would be happy (touchwood). That little innocent boy with his little face and cute smile, who didn't know what kind of world he was getting into, he just looked…amazing."

Jackie looks at me but is lost in thought. He's missing his family but has just given one example of how anything can trigger a memorable moment or memory, which is exactly what his new film is all about. The doting dad, the loving husband, as I eye the time and begin to wrap up my rap-session with the star I wonder if he realises one of the reasons he feels so close to this role is probably because it lets him be who he is: a real family man.

Jackie is currently in Bangalore shooting until the early hours of the morning for the psychological thriller that is Sandhya. His latest release Lajja is doing well at the box office and can be seen at cinemas nationwide.

Fuad Omar

FILM REVIEW: DEVDAS

***ing Shah Rukh Khan, Madhuri Dixit and Aishwarya Rai**
Director: Sanjay Leela Bhansali

Sanjay Leela Bhansali's Devdas is not only a visual masterpiece but a film that is full of love, longing and raw passionate emotions. From the opening shots alone the camera (in a long take) adopts the position of a ghostly presence in the film through whose eyes you witness the events and love unfold. The first thing that strikes you is Binod Pradhan's masterful camerawork that sweeps and rises above shots, creating atmosphere and hovering like watchful eyes over the two families that are central to the story of doomed love that continues to keep promise.

Devdas's story is, simply put, of a man who loves but does not get to be with the one he loves. So deep is his affection that he begins his descent down a self-destructive path, not knowing life without his beloved who he has grown up with. I'll let other reviewers divulge the story, too much has been written about it anyway, I'd rather concentrate on the film and its merits, and the performances.
The narrative structure of the film is seamless, and void of any redundant comedy tracks, token songs or side–storylines that distract from what is central to the plot, which is essentially the love of Devdas for Paro. The script and dialogues are wonderful. It is rare in Indian cinema to find such a quotable film such as Devdas. Be it references to how 'no-one turns to drink for salvation' or the moon descending on earth; Devdas's dialogues are to die for. Couple good dialogues with excellent delivery and

execution courtesy of ace thespian Shah Rukh Khan or Aishwarya Rai or Madhuri Dixit and you have scenes that haunt you, their dialogues echoing in your mind long after the film is over. The way the story, atmosphere and lighting are in sync are superb. How the scene is lit dictates where it's heading in a way never-before seen in Hindi cinema. Be it the bright exterior cuts or the interior confines of a bedroom or lakeside rendezvous, lamps are always present and the manner in which characters faces are brought to life with the use of lighting is simply brilliant. The background score too beats in tune with the film, with each crescendo steering your breaths' staccato and informing each one at what pace to exhale. So haunting is the background score, it reminded me of The Godfather theme, which stirs memories and a feel that cannot be associated with any other film. It has that kind of an aura surrounding it.

Performance-wise Shah Rukh Khan has excelled like never before, venturing into new territory breaking barriers where acting is concerned. Such intensity, raw passion, longing, love and desolation has yet to be seen on the big screen, as is portrayed by the one man wonder that has single-handedly revolutionised Indian cinema. His portrayal of the journey undertaken by Devdas from a romantic lover with a temper to the outcast son who knows nothing but pain, drink and memories gone is breathtaking, compelling and par excellence. His stature and the way he carries himself from his introduction scene alone throws you into Devdas's world, so in no time you understand the character and where he's coming from. This is without a doubt Shah Rukh's most romantic and violent film to date. Romantic, because the hero is a failed one who seeks triumph in his falling and what he feels for Paro is a universal and extremely intense love that leads to his own destruction.

Devdas is without a shadow of doubt the epitome for die-hard romantics everywhere, who will no doubt relate to him in some way or the other. It's also Shah Rukh's most violent film to date because it completely massacres your emotions. The gut-wrenching performance weaves silently into your heart then begins to spontaneously combust with broken glass that cuts with each trouble the fateless lover experiences. By the end of the film, the Devdas we see is not the same one that was introduced. It is a fallen man who has read his own funeral rites, become physically weaker and incapable and has broken down in every way physically and emotionally because of how much he feels for one girl. Shah Rukh's intense and devastatingly shattering performance leaves a mark on Indian cinema that will surely be looked back on for decades to come. Among the highlights are all his scenes with Aishwarya and Madhuri, the confrontational scenes with his father (whether he is present or not) and the drunken stupor he portrays so elegantly and realistically of a man who is in that state because of a crushed and massacred heart. Delivering an award winning performance, Devdas is definitely Shah Rukh's finest hour to date, proving there's so much more to the man who has been consistently questioned after any one film does not match critical expectations.

Aishwarya Rai has yet again come up trumps with a performance that is as subdued as Nandini was extroverted in Bhansali's last film Hum Dil De Chuke Sanam. Her character is much more difficult to play than any of her previous on-screen incarnations, as it requires a depth of understanding of the history of her character, the background and traditions of the family. Then she must emote and react to all around her as one of that background would while playing a resilient, wanting lover to Devdas who must not only display naïveté and simplicity, but also empowerment and grandeur, while consistently walking with grace. Such a role is as complex to describe as it is to assay, and so Devdas's Paro is a role that is an extremely challenging one…a challenge Aishwarya rises to and meets head on, effortlessly displaying why her name will be etched in history forever as Paro's pain is reflected through her glazed and inferno-ridden eyes showing love, anguish, respect and the burden of responsibility. Much has been written about Aishwarya's acting credentials and this film nails the coffin of detractors firmly shut, as she not only matches every gaze of Shah Rukh's with equal intensity (but more subdued in tune with the character), but also matches histrionics with a legend of Indian cinema, Madhuri Dixit.

Madhuri's role of the courtesan who falls for the man who's hopelessly intoxicated on love and his first flame, while breaking out of a cocoon created around her, purpose-built to trap her and her view of the world since an early age is by far one of her most daring roles to date. Madhuri fans will not only be taken aback but delighted with her performance that oozes a mesmerising magic that only Madhuri has captured and held for over a decade. Her screen presence with Shah Rukh is spellbinding and her moments with Aishwarya are a dream. Seeing the two screen beauties together, both who hold great capabilities and talent and have worked their way into celluloid appreciation, one is reminded of how natural the progression is of the Hindi film heroine. At any one time in

Indian cinema, there has only been one actress who has captivated and become the quintessential heroine for that period and Devdas shows how Aishwarya will carry on wherever Madhuri leaves off. Both are vessels of talent that have an untapped reservoir within them, bound only by the restrictions of a role, and both have proved time and again they can create cinematic magic. Madhuri may have less screen-time than Aishwarya and may not be the central character, but her pivotal Chandramukhi is charming and a great balancing factor in the film and characters' lives. She aptly delivers a once-in-a-lifetime performance in a role that allows scope to make each of the twenty four frames that pass per second hers, while she dominates the screen.

Nitin Desai's sets are a feast for the eyes, intoxicating the audience as much as Shah Rukh's character indulges in on-screen. The palace, the stairs, the pillars and the lights, all appear in an all-too-real-looking world that makes you wonder if you really are living in the right side of town. The costumes are heavy and glittery, Madhuri's Benarus saris and Ash's traditionally bordered Dhakai cotton saris adorning each beauty while adding glow to both actresses. Direction by Sanjay Leela Bhansali pays attention to detail be it in the environment or in the character traits. Bhansali has dared to dream an epic on celluloid and successfully transcribes his vision from imagination to big screen in what really is a grand saga of timeless love. The saga tells the story of a man, a woman and fate. Destiny ensures the man's unfulfilled love ends in a timeless manner that will immortalise it forever. Devdas is a film that's intense, emotionally driven and packed full with feasts for the eye and laden with top performances that rank in the finest of Indian cinema history. Witness for yourself the love, the pain and the salvation. Cinema doesn't get any better than this.

Fuad Omar

Acknowledgements:
With very special thanks to my family (especially my parents who I owe everything to), friends, all interviewees, the entire Indian film industry, the readers, those who wrote in and the publications which allowed my work to find its way into the public domain without compromising creative control.

To Bollywood (the greatest film industry in the world): Thank you… for everything.

Fuad Omar
May 2006